COMPLETE
BATHROOM DESIGN

QUARRY

30 Floor Plans; Plus Fixtures, Surfaces, and
Storage Ideas from the Experts

COMPLETE
BATHROOM DESIGN

GLOUCESTER MASSACHUSETTS

QUARRY BOOKS

Holly Harrison
& Sarah Lynch

First published in the United States of America by
Quarry Books, a member of
Quayside Publishing Group
33 Commercial Street
Gloucester, Massachusetts 01930-5089
Telephone: (978) 282-9590
Fax: (978) 283-2742
www.rockpub.com

Library of Congress Cataloging-in-Publication Data available

ISBN 1-59253-201-2

10 9 8 7 6 5 4 3 2 1

Design: Stoltze Design
Cover: Björg/Chelsea Atelier Architects
Spine: Brian Vanden Brink/Steven M. Foote, FAIA, Perry Dean
Rogers Partners
Back cover: Cristian Molina/ColePrévost, Inc., (left); Joy von
Tiedemann/Cecconi Simone, Inc. (right)
Peter Malinowski/DesignARC Architects, (back jacket flap)

Printed in China

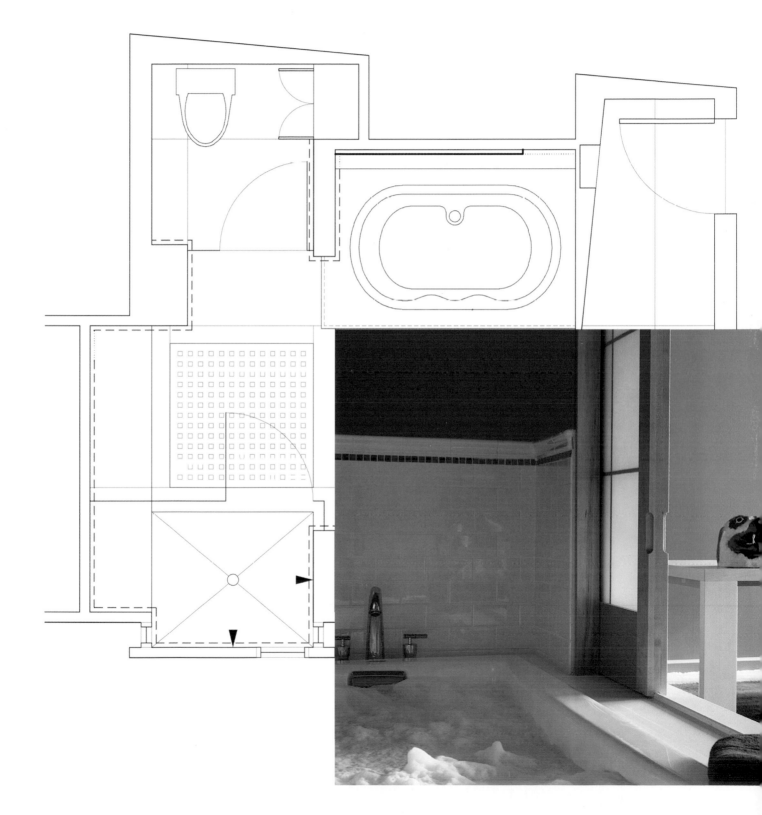

CONTENTS

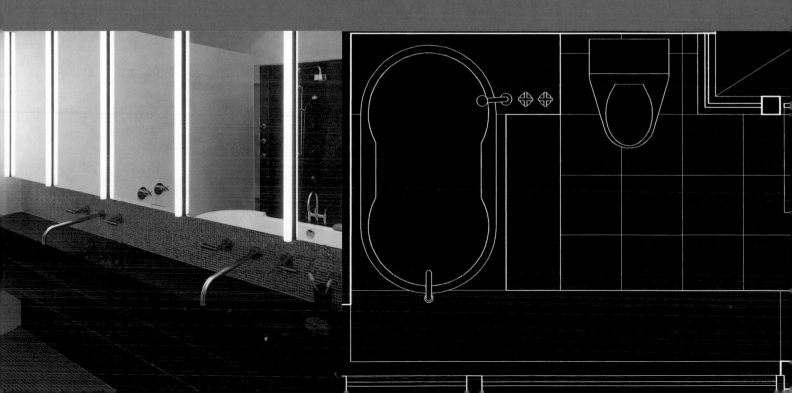

INTRODUCTION

If you are reading this book, you have probably recognized the importance of a spacious, well-designed, and stylish bathroom. Undoubtedly, you have envied your neighbor's oversized bathtub and lusted after those sybaritic retreats published in shelter magazines.

You may freely admit that if you had the bathroom of your dreams, you would spend countless hours there and, if possible, rarely leave. Well, you are not alone.

Even if you've never entertained visions of the perfect bathroom, you have probably dreamed of a better one. The vivid memory of mornings spent showering in cramped stalls, maneuvering around ill-conceived layouts, and stepping onto musty carpeting can inspire in even the most practical homeowner visions of fantasy fixtures and imagined spa amenities, such as lofty ceilings, luxurious surfaces, a heated floor, or a breathtaking view from a huge tub. This is not to say that everyone has the perfect floor plan drawn up or a specific style in mind, but most of us have collected a lifetime of design don'ts that we vow to amend when creating our ideal bathroom. No more brown-and-yellow color schemes. No more flimsy attachments designed to turn a charming tub into an ineffective shower. No more surprise mirrors lurking opposite the toilet or shower door. But a definite yes to such luxuries as a Japanese-style soaking tub, a glass-enclosed shower lined with iridescent mosaic tiles, a mirrored vanity, vintage Art Deco light fixtures, and a clean-lined chaise upholstered in white terry cloth.

The bathroom has come a long way since it was first introduced in the late-19th century. What began as an amenity enjoyed only by the wealthy in their sprawling Gilded Age estates had become the norm by the 1920s, when indoor plumbing was more widely available. At that time, bathrooms were designed for a singular purpose: the hygiene of families in an industrially gritty and disease-ridden era. Stark, white hospital tiles and simple porcelain fixtures were meant to reflect this sanitary sensibility. But human nature cannot live for long without embellishment: The 1930s and '40s saw the introduction of style and decor, with patterned wallpaper and matching bath accessories. By the '50s, color-coordinated fixtures in peachy pinks and sea-foam greens appeared, designed in accordance with the "futuristic" lines of the period. The 1960s and '70s brought even more personalized style into the bathroom: funky textiles, artwork, mirrored wallpaper, and colorful, fuzzy toilet-seat and tissue-box covers. And the opulence of the '80s gave rise to a new focus on design and decorating with bold graphics or themed decors that included matching suites of towels, rugs, accessories, and artwork.

But it was not until the 1990s and the 21st century that the architecture and technology of bathrooms began to catch up with the need for a complete redesign. With a growing focus on health, beauty, and serenity, there was a significant shift in the role bathrooms played in the home. Now, whirlpool tubs, massaging showerheads, overhead heat lamps, and even annexed spaces for exercise equipment are practically considered essentials. Spa retreats, Eastern relaxation techniques, and a return to natural materials have become a part of our consciousness. The healing properties of water are exalted as never before and sold in bottles, fountains, vacations, and, above all, the spa bathroom.

For designers, architects, and do-it-yourselfers alike, the dream of a smart, spacious, stylish bathroom that's customized to meet a person's every need has become a reality. Over the past decade, new homes and renovations have focused on updating the standards of the modern bath so that it meets the demands of our modern lifestyle— one that requires a special place for getting away from the pressures of everyday life, a place for long baths and therapeutic showers, at-home spa treatments, and unhurried morning rituals. The "new" bathroom—considerably larger, more carefully designed, and infinitely more efficient—has become as much a part of our living space as dining rooms, kitchens, and family rooms.

As you will see in the projects included in this book, there are an infinite number of ways to create a beautiful bathroom design—from a small but smart bath that offers Web-surfing from the tub to a 30' (9.1 m)-long oasis with separate activity zones, a Roman-style tub, and a large window wall overlooking a private canyon. Organized to be a useful resource as well as an inspiration and idea generator, this book is divided into three sections to guide you in designing your own functional, stylish, and dreamworthy bathroom. The first section is a sourcebook of every conceivable bathroom component—fixtures, fittings, materials, furnishings, lighting, and upgrades—along with tips to help you pare down the options. The second section showcases 30 bathroom projects and features the designers' or architects' own words of advice on how to make the ideas your own. The final section is a resource guide with phone numbers, contact information, and, when available, websites for every profession, service, and product in the book.

Whether it's simply our changing notions about bathing or a reflection of our decreasing levels of modesty, the bathroom has been opened up to the rest of the home and is, in turn, being designed with equal concern for style and convenience. As a result, it can be customized to perfection without the fear of seeming overly extravagant. We can all use the pampering and luxury of a dream bathroom. Far more than a place to simply wash up, the ideal bathroom is about living, relaxing, relieving stress, beautifying, and feeling healthy, pampered, and, above all, clean.

SECTION ONE:
FIXTURES, FITTINGS, MATERIALS, AND MORE

Designing an ideal bathroom is a kind of balancing act: On the one hand, functionality is paramount. You want the layout to be workable, the fixtures to be comfortable and easy to use, and the lighting to be flattering yet efficient. On the other hand, the ambiance of the environment is also important. As people are spending more time using their bathrooms as retreats and sanctuaries, more care is being put into how the space feels. Is it welcoming? Are the surfaces beautiful to the eye and inviting to the touch? Is there enough storage to keep clutter at bay, and is it integrated into the space without being obtrusive?

This first section of the book gets down to the nitty-gritty, focusing on planning and summarizing the vast world of options available for fixtures, fittings, and materials. Such recent trends as above-counter sinks, designer bathtubs, and heated, sculptural towel warmers are discussed as well as new developments in materials, including ecofriendly ones that are environmentally responsible while still beautiful in their own right.

Getting to know your options is the first step toward figuring out which elements belong on your must-have list and which ones need to be set aside for the sake of a good overall design. Knowing that a wall-mounted sink or toilet makes a room look more streamlined helps if you have a small bathroom to renovate or are trying to achieve a clean-lined contemporary look, regardless of the size of the space. Maybe you'll find that a designer suite of matching furniture is perfect for you, or maybe you'll learn that what you really want is to pick and choose from various sources for a more eclectic look. When you're planning your design, the key is to get out there and look: at other people's bathrooms, at pictures in shelter magazines and design books, at showroom displays. Once you have a notebook filled with photos and ideas and a box filled with samples and swatches, you'll be ready to begin.

The showroom at Urban Archaeology offers a glimpse into the wide array of beautiful materials available for designing the bathroom of your dreams.

PLANNING

Whether you're working with an architect or designer or doing everything yourself, the key to creating a usable and attractive bathroom is planning. Before you immerse yourself in fantasies of honed-limestone tiles, wooden soaking tubs, and radiant heat flooring, you'll need to take a long, hard look at what you're working with.

SPACE

The most important consideration is the shape of your space, because it will determine the layout and the size and type of fixtures you can include. If the space is large but you like to feel cozy and enveloped, adding separate chambers for privacy while bathing or using the toilet could address that need. Do you want a multi-jet shower with room for two? If you're not a tub person, do away with it and put that extra square footage into the shower. Is your space long and narrow? Running the plumbing along one wall will streamline the look and keep down your costs. You'll also need to accommodate structural obstacles such as windows, doors, support beams, ceiling height, lighting, and plumbing. The second section of the book is organized by spatial constraints, exactly because they are so important. You can read about 30 different bathroom spaces and how the architects and designers addressed the shape and layout to create elegant bathrooms with good flow, proper lighting, and all the amenities their clients desired.

BUDGET

Another important aspect of design is your budget. How much you can spend will determine the extent of the renovation that's possible as well as the type of fixtures and materials you'll be able to use. If you're just replacing some fixtures and storage to update the look of the bathroom without taking up the floors and moving walls, you should probably budget $5,000 to $7,000. (Do-it-yourselfers can shave a little off the costs because they'll be installing everything themselves.) A major overhaul, on the other hand, can cost as much as $20,000 to $30,000, or possibly more if you're using high-end fixtures and fittings. Once you know your budget, you can start making a checklist of features and fixtures that you'd like to include, with a sense of what's a necessity (child-friendly fittings, a universally designed roll-in shower, or a double-sink vanity

for a shared bathroom) and what's a luxury (radiant heat floors, a steam shower, a Venetian glass chandelier). After that, it's a matter of tweaking the budget, minimizing in some places so you can splash out in others.

FUNCTION

When you are getting close to choosing specific fixtures and fittings, keep a couple of practical things in mind. Clearance is important, especially if anyone in your household has special needs. You need to plan the placement of the sink, bathtub, toilet, bidet, and shower so that you can maneuver around them. Manufacturers can generally provide specific clearance guidelines as can a contractor, architect, or designer. Keep in mind that ceiling height can be an issue: Although a tub is easily tucked under a sloping eave, you want to be sure you're not going to be knocking your head on a beam every time you get in or out. Also important is that you plan your lighting from the very beginning, rather than simply adding a couple of sconces once the bathroom is finished. Proper lighting not only provides light where it's needed, it can also establish the desired mood or atmosphere for your bathroom. Dimmers can make a room more intimate or provide full light when needed. Programmable LED lights make it possible to change the feeling of the space at will. And at the sink, avoid lighting that's placed directly above you as it will cast shadows in your face that make you look tired and interfere with applying makeup and other grooming.

STYLE

Finally, think about style. Start with how you want the space to feel—a hotel bath, a serene spa, a glamorous mirrored extravaganza, a simple 1920s cottage, a masculine space, a feminine space, cozy, lofty. Determining how you want the space to feel will help you figure out what design style is right for you. From there, it's a matter of choosing the fixtures, fittings, materials, and artwork that will best express the mood you want to create. Whether you're drawn to the warm, natural beauty of stone, the slick, industrial style of metal, or the handcrafted, tactile feel of ceramic tiles, countless materials are available to help you create a bathroom that is practical yet personal, efficient yet stylish.

IN FOCUS:
UNIVERSAL ACCESS BATHROOMS

Whether you are in a wheelchair yourself or want to modify your bathroom for guests or aging parents, redesigning a bathroom for wheelchair access doesn't have to mean compromising on the design. Once you know the basics of what you need, you can start to look through the many options for fittings and fixtures that are available until you find ones that are both visually appealing and functionally appropriate.

Standard U.S. doorways are 24" (61 cm) wide, and wheelchairs require a minimum of 32" (81.3 cm), or 36" (91.4 cm) if the chair has to be turned from a hallway. If you are building from scratch instead of remodeling, consider pocket doors that slide completely out of the way. These are available in many designs, including simple wooden panels, shoji-like screens, and doors inset with panes of frosted or clear glass.

Wall-mounted sinks are ideal for wheelchair access because they can be installed at any height and offer generous clearance below the basin. Although they are available in a multitude of designs and styles, stick to models with shrouds that hide the plumbing to protect against burns and bumping. Lever handles that can be pushed instead of twisted are best for people with limited hand usage. A higher toilet facilitates access for people in wheelchairs and the elderly. Grab bars are available in many designs and can be gracefully blended with the style of your bathroom.

Showers are the most comfortable option for people in wheelchairs. Prefab acrylic or fiberglass units are available in many sizes and colors and can be installed with shower curtains or panel doors. Another option is to create a roll-in shower, allowing enough clearance for easy entry and exit and room to turn once inside. A current trend in bathroom design is the creation of generously sized showers that are open to the room or separated by barely there glass partitions; these showers could be easily tailored for universal access while providing a luxurious experience for all members of a household. As for fittings, a handheld shower is easy to use when standing or seated. Finally, consider installing a special shower seat that folds against the wall when not in use.

To make bathtubs more accessible for elderly visitors or family members, install grab bars to provide support. These accessories are available in many finishes to coordinate with your fittings. Again, as with the sink, lever handles in the tub are preferable. For wheelchair users who prefer bathing to showering, install tub transfer seats. It is especially important to use honed materials on floors or any surfaces where people will be leaning or putting their weight.

Finally, storage should be low enough to be readily accessible for someone who is seated. Many contemporary designs (and reintroduced modernist pieces) are low-to-the-ground, horizontal units that can provide an accessible solution while still retaining their design integrity.

FIXTURES

SINKS

Because the sink is the most-used fixture in a bathroom, utility is an important consideration, which is one reason that vitreous porcelain has long been a material of choice. A recent trend, however, has been to marry practicality with a design statement (and sometimes to disregard function altogether and embrace pure form). Sinks are being produced in all kinds of new materials and styles: Pedestal sinks have morphed into stainless-steel or glass sculptures, while vanity-integrated sinks are jauntily sitting on top of the counter instead of being mounted underneath. The latter trend has paved the way for introducing new basin shapes—chunky rectangles; flat, round circles; and freeform organic bowls. Also popular is repurposing found vessels such as salad bowls or copper pots. Rather than a basin or bowl, a sink can be a long, flat piece of tempered glass or stainless steel attached to the wall at an angle and plumbed. With so many interesting sink options available today, the hardest part of installation may just be choosing the one you like best.

WALL-MOUNT
A wall-mounted sink works well in a small space because it takes up minimal room, and the pipes can be recessed into the wall for a streamlined appearance. (A wall-mounted sink must be attached to a wall stud.) Most wall-mounts are available with a shroud that hides the pipes, but you can leave them exposed to add a sculptural element. The vivid orange sink shown is a design from Agape and is made of a folded sheet of flexible PVC and supported by a stainless-steel ring.

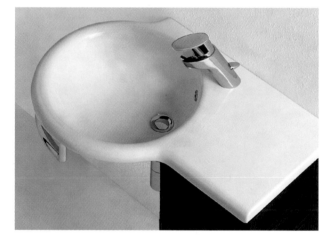

WALL-MOUNT WITH STORAGE
Some wall-mounted models are little more than a tiny basin, while others (such as the Luce 75 from Hastings Bath Collection shown) have such extras as attached towel racks, counter space, and drawers for storage.

LEFT: Integral sinks are physically integrated with the countertop, which can be of vitreous china, cast polymers, fiberglass, and stainless steel (which is welded). The sink/vanity unit has no lips or crevices, which makes it easy to keep clean; it is simply attached to the top of a cabinet or vanity or can be a wall-mount like the Starck 3 from Duravit (which could also be mounted in a custom cabinet).

RIGHT: A longstanding favorite, pedestal sinks do away with bulky vanities and are easy to install. A classic white pedestal sink fits in with any style decor while Mattheo Thun's terra-cotta ceramic Positano design (manufactured by Studio Rapsel) makes a dramatic and colorful modern statement.

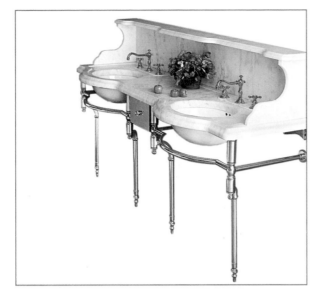

WASHSTANDS
Washstands are freestanding units that are easily integrated into a bathroom. Usually they have a little more storage than a wall-mounted or pedestal sink and are available in classic and contemporary designs. Here, a Victorian washstand in honed white Carrara marble (by Urban Archaeology) mixes decorative historic style with modern amenities such as double sinks and built-in storage.

VANITY WITH UNDERCOUNTER SINK
A sink that's integrated into a vanity has the double advantage of hidden plumbing and plenty of storage. Like furniture, a vanity can be created in any style and can be very simple or quite elaborate. The Archive vanity by Porcher is shown with an oval basin mounted to the underside of the Carrara marble counter for a clean, integrated look.

VANITY WITH SELF-RIMMING SINK
For a sink that's easy to install anywhere, consider a self-rimming basin. At left, the Isis from Gres de Breda's Arlequin line is made of the same ceramic tile as the vanity top while Kohler's stainless-steel Rhythm is set into teak for a crisp, delineated look.

VESSELS
The latest trend in sinks is the above-counter vessel, which can be attached to the top of a vanity cabinet or onto a cantilevered shelf. For a modern look, pair a chunky white or blue basin with a teak countertop. For a cottage-style design, pair a pottery basin with a painted washstand. Kohler's Serpentine Bronze basin brings an exotic look to the bathroom, with its pattern of interlaced serpents based on an ancient Chinese design.

TROUGH SINKS
Trough sinks make a big, bold statement and are a great option where space isn't an issue. They can be installed as wall-mounts, integrated into vanities, or supported by washstands. Agape's long crystal glass basin is shown recessed into the Flat XL cantilevered countertop, which is made of Parapan. A small removable Parapan shelf provides a place for soap and other toiletries. Adding a second faucet allows the piece to act as a double sink for a couple or family.

BATHTUBS

For many people, the tub is the heart of the bathroom—it's where children (or pets) are bathed, bulky winter sweaters are washed, and long, restful soaks are enjoyed. Aesthetically, a beautiful tub can have the presence of a sculpture, especially in a large bathroom, where it can be placed in the center of the room (either freestanding or integrated into a stone, tile, or wood surround) or made the focal point in a smaller space when set against an eye-catching backdrop.

While the cast-iron claw-foot tub is a timeless classic, freestanding tubs have come into their own and are being produced in dozens of styles—from traditional to contemporary, compact to capacious. Advances in technology and the development of heat-retaining, moldable composite materials have opened up bathtub design with the creation of organic shapes and body-hugging forms. The recent popularity of industrial materials has led to the production of metal tubs in classic and modern styles using copper, unfinished cast iron, and stainless steel.

This massive polished-concrete tub was assembled onsite from five tongue-and-groove pieces by Stone Soup Concrete, a company that specializes in concrete projects and serves the New England area. The tub weighs 1,750 lbs. (793.8 kg) and can hold 120 gallons (454.2 liters) of water.

This white freestanding tub may look like a classic, but it's made of Ficore (by Design & Form), a high-tech composite composed of eight materials that was developed specifically for bathtubs. It can withstand temperatures up to 175° F (80° C) and holds heat well. Designed by Michael S. Smith, the Town Bathtub has a lower drain and is equally at home in modern and traditional bathrooms. (Available through Ann Sacks.)

Chefs swear by their copper pots, and now Ann Sacks is offering a bathtub that has the same heat-retaining abilities. Part of the Kuo Collection, it's a handcrafted, freestanding oval with double-wall construction and body-fitting curves. The reddish tones of the metal add warmth to the bath, which seems to fit in naturally with its stone surroundings.

This handsome design by renowned architect Sir Norman Foster offers contemporary looks and classic appeal. As shown, the dark wooden surround contrasts crisply with the linear quality of the pure white tub, emphasizing the clean lines of the design. (Available through C.P. Hart.)

Built-in bathtubs have their own set of advantages, especially because they can be integrated into any decor and present the opportunity to use interesting materials such as tile, stone, and wood on the decking or apron. Many standard bathtubs are meant to fit into a three-walled alcove, but if you envision a deck around your tub, an undermounted bathtub provides a seamless integration and puts visual emphasis on the surface material used for the deck. Drop-ins are also an option and have the advantage of not requiring a perfect opening because they are self-rimming. Some models come with a raised lip that adds a finished look. Finally, you can simply sink a bathtub into the floor to create your own private pond.

Customizing a bathtub is another option. If you have specific dimensions or a special shape or look in mind, consider building a tub from scratch, but take care in choosing a waterproof design and practical materials. Large, sunken tubs built with honed stone slabs or clad with mosaic tiles can bring the indulgences of a Roman bath into the home while a round, polished-concrete basin can add a touch of whimsy. Keep in mind that heavy bathtubs require strong floors that can handle the weight, so be sure to check with an architect or knowledgeable builder before moving forward.

The Zen Bathtub from Christian Lefroy Brooks's OX line is a serene oval that invites soaking. Shown here with English Oak supports, it can also be installed in a deck.

Originally produced in France during the 19th century, the bateau (or boat) bath tub is now offered by Christian Lefroy Brooks with a polished solid-cast aluminum exterior that doesn't tarnish. The freestanding tub features a center drain, which is more comfortable when sharing.

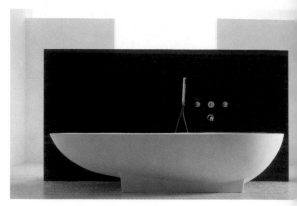

Agape's ergonomic Spoon bathtub is designed for pride of place in the center of the room (though it can be installed next to a wall as well). It looks a bit like a big concrete basin, but it's actually made of Exmar, a heat-retaining composite of resin and quartz powder. Designed by G.P. Benedini, the tub is available with column-mounted tap controls or a simple floor-standing tap.

From Rapsel Studio, Peter Büchele's sleek stainless-steel tub is available in various finishes but is shown here as a study in opposites: The exterior is satiny smooth, and the interior is polished to a high-gloss shine.

If you've got room for it, Michael Graves's big, round Dreamscape tub (from Duravit) adds visual drama while providing plenty of room for splashing around. Although those chunky legs are practically irresistible, it's also available as a drop-in.

The Woodline tub from Agape is made of natural oak plywood inside and out. The strong geometry of the rectangular shape is broken up in the interior with an undulating floor that provides an ergonomic fit for bathers.

This elegant cast-iron slipper tub from Sunrise Specialty features a vitreous porcelain interior and solid brass claw feet with a range of finishes (polished chrome is shown). The bath exterior is primed against rust and finished with a high-gloss white exterior enamel.

IN FOCUS:

SPA-STYLE BATHS

For an at-home spa experience, whirlpool and spa baths can be harmoniously integrated into almost any design style. Three basic types are available: hot tubs that recirculate water and are intended for soaking rather than bathing; tubs that pump warm air into the water; and whirlpool baths, which circulate a mixture of air and water through jets. A hot tub is a good choice for an outdoor bath (on a patio or in a pool house) or for a combined bath/personal gym suite. Air-jet bathtubs from specialty companies such as Ultra Bath (BainUltra) provide massage through dozens of tiny air jets (kind of like an air hockey table). Because the water doesn't circulate through pipes, there's no issue of standing water when the tub is not in use and no need for extra plumbing access, which makes this model an option even in smaller bathrooms. (It takes up the same space as a regular tub.) Whirlpool baths come in a range of colors, shapes, and sizes, and many now include lighting for creating a relaxing atmosphere.

Chromatherapy baths by Kohler use LED lights to color the water in a cycle of eight colors or a single shade when specified. The sök Overflowing Bath shown is designed to soothe the senses with its continual cascade of water over the tub's edges and effervescent bubbles.

A whirlpool bath in an undermount design allows for harmonious integration into any bathroom design. The Tea for Two cast-iron, enameled whirlpool comes with multiple jets and is made by Kohler.

If you don't need the money for a new car, splash out on Jacuzzi's over-the-top La Scala two-person whirlpool. Standard options include: a 42-inch (106.7 cm) high-definition plasma TV monitor, DVD and CD player, surround-sound speakers, video monitoring, and Internet access. Once you settle in, you may just never leave.

SHOWERS

No longer just a showerhead attachment behind a plastic curtain, showers have come into their own as spaces unto themselves with generous proportions, elaborate showerheads (rainmakers, water-falls, and multi-jets), assorted door options, and a seemingly endless array of tile options. Easy to customize, they can be made in any shape or material, as long as they are waterproof and have slip-resistant floors. The first decision you'll need to make is where to put your shower. Many people are separating the bath and shower by installing a tub that's open to the room for soaking and an enclosed niche for showering. Shower curtains can be easily replaced for a style update, but more permanent water barriers include sliding doors, pivot doors, and glass panels that leave room to step in and out. Opaque doors are a popular choice as they add a sense of mystery along with providing more privacy than clear tempered glass. Acrylic modules, which come in various sizes, make it easy to install a separate shower even in a small space. Most are fitted with ledges for toiletries and many come with integral seating and grab bars, making them an excellent choice for universally designed bathrooms. A recent trend has been to do away with wet and dry zones altogether, opening the shower up to create a wet room (see page 48) for a lush, spa-like experience. Finally, shower environments can be fine-tuned with special lighting, piped-in music, and heat lamps installed just outside the door.

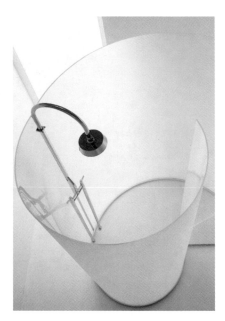

CURVED SHOWER STALL (LEFT)
Its curving methacrylate walls inspired by the shape of a shell, Agape's freestanding Chiocciola shower adds elegance to any bathroom. The spiral can be partially inserted into the wall for a more integrated look.

IN-TUB SHOWER (RIGHT)
Looking like a ship about to set sail, Peter Büchle's whimsical Ima design for Studio Rapsel is also practical, with a rustproof stainless-steel frame and a curtain made of mold-proof fabric.

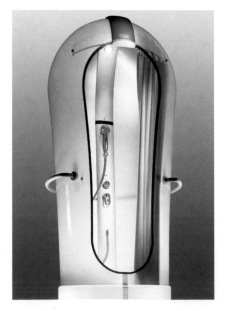

FREESTANDING MODULE (LEFT)
Many new materials are making their way into the shower, from translucent Panelite doors to acrylics in freeform shapes and eye-popping colors. Pharo's freestanding Cocoon is rendered in four colors of translucent acrylic and has an integral lighting system and an attached rail that warms towels while you wash.

BODY SPA (RIGHT)
Kohler's BodySpa 8-Jet System is the shower equivalent of a whirlpool bath: Fill the basin with clean water, then turn it on for an all-over massage. When you're done, just turn it off and let the water drain out. Although it's not intended for washing (the system has to remain soap-free), a regular showerhead can be installed in the same space. For other spa-like showerheads, see page 26.

IN FOCUS:

TRANSPARENT SHOWER

When creating a house for Connecticut clients with a private wooded view, architect Rand Elliot erased the lines between inside and out by building the house with 10' high (304.8 cm) window walls throughout. In the master bath, he created the feel of an outdoor shower by placing a glass shower stall right in front of the window wall. The floor is a slate slab floating above a hidden drain, so that water just runs off the edge of the slab and disappears. Plumbing is hidden in a white marble triangular column that stands like a statue in one corner of the shower. "The technical details of this bath are all well thought out," says Elliot. "They were designed in an effort to hide all of the details that are often accepted but aren't contributing to the quality of the experience." On one wall, a built-in granite-covered bench provides a place to shave your legs, dry off, or just daydream while gazing out the window.

TOILETS AND BIDETS

A number of factors influence the choice of the right toilet: spatial considerations, size and comfort, water-saving options, and, not unimportant, design. Practically speaking, rounded-front toilets are a little more compact and are a good choice for small spaces, while elongated-front ones have an elegant bowl shape and offer added comfort. Some toilets come at a higher-than-standard height, making them a good choice for tall people, older people who might have trouble sitting down, and people in wheelchairs. Children's sizes are also available. A couple of basic structural variations are available: one-piece toilets, which are a seamless unit with no crevices (easy to keep clean); the ubiquitous two-piece toilets, which have a separate tank and bowl that are bolted together on installation; and toilets without visible tanks (the tank is hidden in the wall behind). The latter have a streamlined look and are also available as wall-mounts. Stainless-steel toilets, which are easy to keep clean and don't stain, are moving from public restrooms into the home. Whatever your bathroom's decor, dozens of options, from barely there, sleek, modern pieces to old-fashioned designs with high tanks and pull chains (available through specialty companies), are available in a vast array of colors and seat choices. Lastly, consider heated seats and covers to go with your radiant heat floors for a truly sybaritic experience.

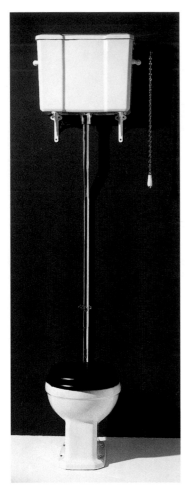

The London porcelain pull-chain toilet is an antique style with modern plumbing. Although this piece makes a charming addition to an old-fashioned bathroom, keep in mind that the high cistern takes up wall space, which makes this a less practical option for small bathrooms. (Available through C.P. Hart.)

Bidets, or sit-down washbasins, are considered more hygienic than toilet paper for both sexes. In-toilet hygiene systems can be installed in a toilet where space in the bathroom is an issue. But where there's room, consider a bidet in a complementary style to your toilet. Here, Alessi's matching bidet and toilet set brings a bold, contemporary look to the bathroom, standing out dramatically against a wall of deep red mosaic tiles. A towel ring hanging nearby makes drying off easy. (Available through C.P. Hart.)

Instead of hiding the tank, some designs embrace it, creating tall, slender versions that rise up the wall to bring a little drama to the bath. Duravit's two-piece Giorno design, by Massimo Iosa Ghini, takes it a step further by adding facets to both tank and bowl for a crystalline look that's so futuristic it takes 21st-century design into the 22nd.

Duravit's lidded home urinal (the Darling is shown) doesn't take up a lot of space and solves the age-old seat-up versus seat-down debate between men and women sharing a bathroom. Designed by Dieter Sieger.

Although wall-mounts are available in all styles, Duravit's unequivocally modern Dreamscape model, designed by Michael Graves, has a chunky square base and rounded bowl for a sculptural look that's interesting and fresh.

An attractive one-piece WC, the L'Expression by Porcher has an elongated front and a tall, slim tank; the chic, modern design would go well in any contemporary home.

FITTINGS

SINK FAUCETS AND TUB FILLERS

Although they perform a much-needed function, bathroom fittings also add sparkle and can act as the finishing touch on your design. Styles range from barely there wall-mounted faucets to elaborate metal sculptures and come in any number of finishes. Polished chrome is a classic choice, but other options include satin and polished variations of gold, brass, bronze, nickel, and stainless steel. When it's possible, choosing the same finish for all metal parts of the sink or tub presents a more unified appearance. Metal surfaces usually require some maintenance—using a nonabrasive cleaner and, in some cases, toweling them dry after use. (Stainless steel is particularly susceptible to water spots.)

Finding the right faucet depends on how you will use it, the physical constraints of your space, and the style of your bathroom. For a house with children or elderly, an electronic faucet that turns itself off and on or one with lever handles that are easy to maneuver would be a good choice. Long popular in kitchens, high-arched faucets are becoming ubiquitous in bathrooms, because they allow more room at the sink for tasks such as filling a bucket for cleaning or hand-washing delicate clothing. For small spaces, minimizing your faucet can make room on the countertop for toiletries. Larger bathrooms offer a chance to play a little, with decorative finials, wide or tall faucets, and double sinks.

Artfully combining ceramic and brushed nickel, Kohler's one-handled Bol faucet is decorated with a pattern inspired by Japanese silk-screened fabrics.

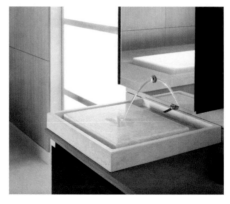

This magical faucet is so minimal that the water seems to flow right out of the wall. Made by Kohler, the Laminar Flow faucet can be wall or ceiling mounted. It is pictured here with the Purist Wet Surface Lavatory.

Dornbracht's Meta Plasma faucet by Dieter Sieger adds a pop of vivid color to any sink or vanity; the lever mixer comes in three bold hues—orange, frog green, and blue. It is available for bidets as well.

Shown here in polished nickel, this jaunty pair of Victorian basin pillar taps from Hollys of Bath has cross handles with stylish porcelain insets that read *Hot* and *Cold* and a matching drain plug.

Under the direction of designer Stefano Giovannoni, Alessi has produced a line of bathroom fixtures that puts the emphasis on elemental shapes: round basins and a minimal faucet that's just a pure, straight line.

Vola's wall-mounted faucet brings stylish utility to a whole new level. The one-handled mixer has a double-swivel spout that can be pushed to the side when extra room is needed at the sink.

Hollys of Bath carries a Victorian bath shower mixer that is just right for an old-fashioned claw-foot tub. It is shown in an antique gold finish and comes with a cradle, hand-shower set, and a floor-mount with standing legs.

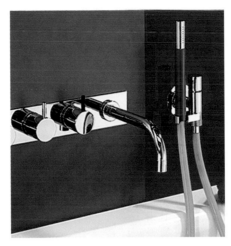

This sleek, wall-mounted Vola faucet, shown in polished chrome, has a two-handled mixer and a handheld shower attachment that's a stylish wand.

With a wide base and high-arched curve, Kohler's graceful tub-mounted Taboret faucet has a high-flow capacity that's good for extra-large tubs and whirlpool baths but doesn't look clunky or oversized.

Philippe Starck designed this single-lever faucet for Axor. With its angled faucet and rounded lever, the unit (shown in polished chrome) is minimalist yet also dynamic. (Available through C.P. Hart.)

At home in modern or traditional settings, Kohler's tub-mounted Memoirs Classic faucet makes a suitable companion for almost any standard-size bathtub. Shown in brushed nickel, it's available with lever or cross handles.

The perfect mate for an old-fashioned slipper or claw-foot tub, Sunrise Specialty's Tubfill handheld shower mounts through the bathtub rim with the aid of a tower drain. The faucet and waste are both self-supporting, making it possible to install the tub anywhere your pipes will go.

Vanity- or basin-mounted sink faucets come in one-handled versions with a single lever that pushes right or left for temperature control, one-handled or two-handled faucets with escutcheon plates, and widespread designs that require separate holes for the faucet and handles. If you are simply replacing your faucets rather than installing a whole new sink, you'll need to be sure you have the right kind for the holes that are already there (a single hole or three that are either close or wide set). Another popular option is a wall-mounted faucet, which requires a separate wall-mount valve and drain but works well with vanity/sink combos such as undermounted basins or above-counter vessels.

Tubs can be served by wall-mounted and tub- or deck-mounted faucets as well as (for freestanding ones) floor-mounted versions with a tower drain. Some faucets for antique tubs are not self-supporting and require extra support from brackets attached to a wall, which may limit your room layout. For any mounting, you want to be sure that the faucet extends forward enough. Keep in mind that oversized tubs and whirlpool baths take a long time to fill so you'll want to choose a high-flow model. For tubs that are large enough for sharing, installing the faucet in the middle will allow both people to lean back without the fittings getting in the way.

SHOWERHEADS

Not only are showerheads available in a wide range of styles and finishes, but shower technology has developed from a science to an art, so that people can fine-tune their shower experience to be relaxing or invigorating, simple or complex. This is all done through the choice and installation of showerheads. There are five basic types: fixed (generally mounted on the wall at a height of about 78" [198.1 cm]), handheld, handheld on a slide bar, ceiling-mounted, and multiple-jet systems, which are composed of showerheads and spray jets in some combination.

Water temperature is controlled through pressure-balancing faucets (which respond to changes in water pressure) or thermostatic faucets (which respond to changes in water pressure and temperature changes in the water supply). Thermostatic showers are available with single- or dual-thermostatic controls. The former requires the bather to twist a single control to adjust water flow and temperature, while the latter addresses the two functions with separate dials. Some models allow you to preset the desired temperature so that when you turn on the water, it's exactly right for you. Showerheads are also available with two control handles, one for hot and one for cold water, just like a sink or tub faucet.

LEFT: Still in the project stage, Sieger Design's Overhead Rain Shower Spray System for Dornbracht re-creates the experience of falling rain for a beautiful shower. An electronic control unit will set the temperature and allow the water flow to be chosen from among three proposed rain types: monsoon, country, and summer.

RIGHT: Adjustable to many heights along the slide bar, this wall-mounted single-lever shower mixer can also act as a handheld shower. The sleek design by Dieter Sieger is fittingly called Oasis (from the Meta.02 line) and is manufactured by Dornbracht. Shown in polished chrome, it is also available in matte platinum.

LEFT: Pan-head showers are also called rain-making or needle-head showers because they mimic rainfall. They are available as wall- or ceiling-mounted models and range in size from 8 to 12" (20.3 to 30.5 cm). The Waterloo Easyclean8 shower rose with the C.P. Hart arm is available through C.P. Hart.

RIGHT: This clever unit from Hansgrohe is a flat, wall-mount shower panel (#26680001) complete with overhead showerhead, a handheld shower, thermostatic mixer, and four adjustable body sprays that can turn almost any shower setup into a spa experience.

Handheld sets are gaining popularity as a second showerhead, one that can be used for washing children, rinsing feet, or cleaning the shower walls. Handheld showers can also be installed to slide along a stationary vertical bar, so that the height of the showerhead can be easily tailored to all household members.

Adjustable-spray showerheads provide a range of spray options, from gentle and aerated to pulsating and massaging. Extra-wide or pan-head showerheads are a recent trend and can be installed on the wall or from the ceiling for an experience similar to rinsing in the rain. Also on the rise is the use of multiple-jet showers, which spray the bather from all angles for a lavish, invigorating wash. If you don't want to open up the wall to put in an elaborate shower system, one option is to install a wall-mounted shower panel with integrated jets. Another is to install a freestanding thermostatic shower cage. Waterworks offers one that features a series of water sprays set in a curved armature. In the end, the showerhead you choose will depend in part on the limitations of your water pressure and plumbing codes. In general, it's a good idea to consult with a plumber or builder before making a major change.

ACCESSORIES

Many collections of fittings from designers or manufacturers come with a matching line of accessories, such as towel bars, toothbrush holders, toilet paper holders, and hooks to create a fully integrated look for the bathroom.

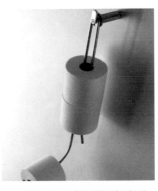

From Alessi, this wall-mounted toothbrush holder doesn't take up precious counterspace and won't get knocked off the vanity by the cat. The clear container pulls out of the chrome holder to facilitate cleaning.

Dieter Sieger's clever toilet paper holder, from Dornbracht's Meta.02 line, may very well solve the problem of husbands (or wives) not replacing a used-up roll—simply lift off the old, drop on the new.

Agape's designers found inspiration in a simple paper clip when creating this functional and attractive toilet paper roll holder. A bent, sprung, satin steel rod, which can be unhooked from the wall attachment, provides storage and easy access for to up to three rolls.

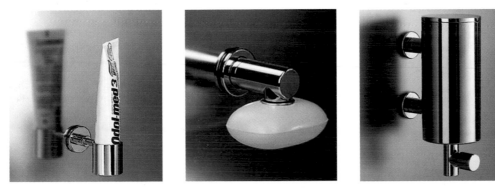

Some of Vola's handy bathroom extras include a wall-mounted toothpaste tube holder, soap magnet, and soap/shampoo dispensers available in 2-pint and 1-pint (1- and 0.5-liter) sizes.

MATERIALS

STONE AND TILE

Easy to care for, long-lasting, and available in a mind-boggling array of materials and colors, tile is perfect for a bathroom. The nearly infinite palette and variety of tiles available will allow you to get creative with color combinations, patterns, and designs. This versatile material can be used on floors, walls, vanities, and showers and as cladding for sink and tub basins. You can even install it yourself, if you are handy. (The Home Depot offers workshops that can teach you the basics in a couple of hours.) Whether you're installing tiles yourself or hiring someone, there's a world of tile available that can help you establish the mood you want in your bathroom, whether it's a tranquil stone oasis or a sleek, glass-covered spa.

Because it's an investment to tile a bathroom, you'll want to consider your options carefully. If you're the kind of person who likes to follow trends, you might want to go with a neutral tile choice and add color and variation through towels and accessories that can be more easily and frequently changed. If, however, you want to make more of a statement, a whole bathroom done in a vivid tile color or a bold mosaic pattern can be stunning. Also consider your lifestyle (and be honest with yourself). While solid colors carry a lot of punch, mottled tiles will be more forgiving in terms of showing dust or smudges. And in colder climates, you may want to consider radiant heat, which works beautifully with tile floors, keeping them toasty warm underfoot.

AS YOU START TO PLAN YOUR RENOVATION, KEEP IN MIND A FEW BASICS:

Size: While the most popular tile remains the 4 ¼" (11.4 cm) square wall tile, the current trend is toward larger sizes, especially 12 x 12" (30.5 x 30.5 cm). Large tiles make a room seem larger and have less grout to keep clean. For floors, they are available in honed, slip-resistant finishes. At the other end of the spectrum, ¾" (1.9 cm) mosaic tiles are an appealing choice as the small, repeated squares create a geometric presence. The extra grout lines also increase grip on floors.

Ceramic: Most ceramic tiles are glazed and come in glossy, matte, and slip-resistant surfaces. Many manufacturers offer relief patterns for borders that coordinate with tiles and make an attractive feature along a wall or counter edge.

Stone: Available in slab and tile form, slate, marble, granite, limestone, and travertine add a rich natural beauty to the bathroom. Some stones such as limestone are warm, while others such as granite are cool to the touch. If you're working with a smaller budget but want to have some stone in your bathroom, consider limiting it to thresholds and windowsills or using it on a single surface such as a vanity or tub decking. Also, there are many tiles on the market that mimic the look of stone and are much less expensive. Keep in mind that slabs are heavy, so they need proper support on floors and walls.

Mosaic: Mosaic tiles are available in glass and clay versions. The clay ones are pigmented so that the color goes all the way through the tile. They can be used on almost any surface and are waterproof, stainproof, and extremely sturdy. Mosaic tiles usually come in 12 x 12" (30.5 x 30.5 cm) sheets and can be customized to your design specifications or purchased in ready-made color combinations by manufacturers such as Bisazza.

Quarry: A deep red unglazed tile used mostly for interior floors, quarry tiles are highly porous— probably not an ideal choice for a bathroom, though they can be sealed.

Shapes: Rectangular, hexagonal, diamond, square, circular—tiles are available in many shapes. Most lines also have trim tiles designed for borders, corners, and accents. These embellishments will add a finished, professional look to your installation.

Grout: Grouts are available in many colors and can be used in their own right as an accent color or to create a harmonious blend.

1 French Metro ceramic tiles (Urban Archaeology); 2 Capri ceramic tiles (Ann Sacks); 3 Gasgone bluestone slab (Walker Zanger); 4 Brushed Alloy stainless-steel tiles (Ann Sacks); 5 Gaudi glass mosaic tiles (Emaux de Briare); 6 Cobalt ceramic tile with a semi-gloss finish (Dal-Tile); 7 Positano Auriella pattern in limestone (Ann Sacks); 8 South Beach ceramic tiles (Ann Sacks); 9 St.Tropez Pebbles travertine tile in champagne (Ann Sacks); 10 Flies Eyes hexagonal ceramic tiles with Belfry crackled-glass border tiles (Urban Archaeology); 11 Lake Scene ceramic tile (Urban Archaeology); 12 Picolo marble tiles (Urban Archaeology); 13 Dana's Glass in the snail pattern (Ann Sacks); 14 Victorian Border ceramic tile (Urban Archaeology); 15 Kasbah pattern ceramic mosaic tiles in oasis green (Walker Zanger); 16 Pergola ceramic border tile (Walker Zanger).

WOOD

There's nothing quite like the organic presence of wood in a home, but when it comes to the bathroom, there's the tricky issue of possible water damage. Although many types of hardwoods are more water-resistant than others, all wood requires extra care and maintenance to stay beautiful in a bathroom, whether it's used as a building material or for accent furnishings.

For larger rooms that can be separated into wet and dry zones, wood furniture adds warmth and character. Customizing an antique hutch with a sink basin can create a charming and unique vanity. Additionally, wooden vanities topped by marble slabs, a synthetic material such as Corian, tiles, or metal can be purchased or custom made. For those who are nervous about water damage for wood furniture, flooring, or tub decking, numerous sealers are available that can waterproof wood without changing the appearance of the grain or its luster. Wood has a flexible nature and can be either warm or cool, depending on the color and stain treatment—a deep reddish mahogany warms a space, while a pickled wood or light ash adds coolness. Finally, some companies have begun to experiment with wood as a material for making sinks and bathtubs. For example, Agape has created an intriguing line of wooden sinks and bathtubs (called Woodline) using molded plywood. (The tub is shown on page 18.)

To bring wood safely into the bathroom as a structural element such as paneling or flooring, you'll want to keep in mind a couple of things. Some woods are naturally water-resistant—teak, for example, can take a soaking, which is why it's used on boats and for outdoor furniture. With its reddish tones, it's a beautiful choice for vanities, cabinets, in-shower benches, permanent bath mats, and molding for doors and windows in wet zones. Exotic woods such as Hinoki cedar, traditionally used to make Japanese soaking tubs, and African iroko are rot-resistant and can be used to make beautiful sinks. For softer wood varieties such as pine, there's the issue of wood's tendency to expand and contract as temperatures fluctuate and the possibility of warping due to water damage. Because wood is a costly investment, it's wise to consult a professional before plunging in.

Finally, consider going green: Renewable wood sources such as bamboo, which replenishes itself in four years, make for attractive, ecologically responsible flooring and are increasingly available. (The Home Depot Design Expo stocks bamboo floors.) Additionally, wood salvaged from old barns and houses has character and can be used for flooring or custom furnishings.

To create a working sink in a bathroom that also houses a washer and dryer, architect Amelie Rennolds and designer Frits Drescher collaborated on a deep teak basin with a flip-down shelf for folding laundry. "There's no finish on the teak; it's just oiled," says Rennolds. "Every now and then we sand it down and oil it again." Although it requires extra care, a wooden sink evokes a tactile, water-on-wood experience that connects us to elements in nature, such as water hitting a fallen log or rain collected in a barrel or tree stump.

FABRIC AND WALLPAPER

Fabric and wallpaper bring warmth to a bathroom as well as a world of texture and color. Cotton and terry cloth are especially suitable bathroom fabrics (and consequently popular) because they are easy to wash and are naturally absorbent. Sailcloth and canvas are both sturdy and are a good choice for shower curtains or upholstered pieces. Placing looped-pile rugs by the tub and sink adds color and texture while also keeping puddles from forming. Where privacy isn't an issue, consider organza sheers in the window to diffuse the light without blocking it. Terry cloth towels in assorted colors enliven a space and help bathers keep track of which is theirs (especially useful for large families) while a stack of fluffy white towels evokes a hotel or spa atmosphere. When towels get old and frayed, replace them with something different—it's the least expensive way to renovate your bathroom.

Wallpapers featuring natural grass, gold-leaf squares, or printed patterns are just some of the artful options available that can help define and personalize a space. Half baths are an ideal place for wallpaper, as the lack of a steamy shower makes for better adhesion.

Adding lively color to this small bathroom are two fabrics by Zimmer + Rohde: The shade is made of a design called Parfum and the screen below it is covered with Lumière.

GLASS

With its shimmering depths and availability in virtually any color, glass is a wonderful addition to a bathroom. Because it's not style-specific, a pane of glass (in this form, it should always be laminated or tempered for safety) can be combined with almost any palette and design style, making it a good choice for unobtrusive shower panels. For privacy and mystery, glass can be sandblasted or acid-etched until it is opaque and placed in sliding-door panels, entry doors, and even windows where privacy is key. Decoratively, it can be attached to walls in panel form or as tiles. (The only drawback to glass is that it requires extra care, such as using a rubber squeegee on shower stalls or wiping down tiled surfaces to avoid spots.) Available in many sizes, glass tiles are especially popular in the 1" (2.5 cm) mosaic size and can be used to cover any surface in the bathroom: floor-to-ceiling in showers, in bathtub basins, on shelving, on vanity tops, as wainscoting, on floors, and even to line a sink.

All of the decorative elements in this spacious bathroom are created from mosaic tiles: There's a "carpet," yellow "wainscoting," and a floorboard that's implied by the green-and-white stripe running along the bottom of the wall. (From SICIS Mosaic & Art.)

These fascinating glass tiles fuse new technology with Czech glass-craft traditions. Called Live Tiles, they contain light-refracting patterns that create a kind of 3-D, shimmering effect. Available (to the trade) in eight standard formats and two thicknesses, Live Tiles can be used on various interior and exterior surfaces.

Two sinks demonstrate the versatility of glass (from left): Nost from Studio Rapsel is a sleek, green shelf of tempered glass while Porcher's Rock Ice basin is a vivid blue bowl that's smooth on the inside and nubby on the outside.

To create Nymphaea, a line of chroma-therapeutic vessel sinks, Lotus Aquatech integrated temperature-sensitive LED lights with the glass so that the basins change color, depending on the temperature of the water hitting them. (Available through the Whitehaus Collection.)

INDUSTRIAL

Concrete and a range of metals are being integrated into modern bathrooms in creative and beautiful ways that belie their industrial origins. Influenced by the recent renaissance of modernist design, the guts of construction are reappearing in the form of exposed steel support beams and poured-concrete walls. But a slew of new products is available as well: Polished concrete, a popular flooring option (which can be heated), is also being used to make countertops, sinks (both integrated and poured into round and square vessels), and even bathtubs. Any number of decorative finishes are available: from a soft, tactile matte to super glossy, intricately stenciled designs to an acid-etched surface that can look like stone or marble. Stainless steel, long appreciated for its sturdiness for sinks, is now being embraced as decoration: Walker Zanger, Ann Sacks, and Artistic Tile all carry lines of stainless-steel tiles with designs ranging from flat, polished mosaics to tiles with raised geometric surface patterns. For a warmer look, lustrous copper is available in many applications from paneling to basins and tubs.

Syndecrete is a precast concrete made with recycled aggregates developed by architect David Hertz (founder of Syndesis, Inc.) as an alternative to limited or nonrenewable natural materials and petroleum-based synthetics. Recycled materials such as glass chips, metal shavings, and plastic regrinds make up 41 percent of the material and give it the appearance of a funky terrazzo.

Behind the sink, a steely gray backsplash of stainless-steel mosaic tiles by Ann Sacks brings a look of industrial chic to the bathroom.

A soft, green countertop installed by Stone Soup Concrete softly complements this simple white vessel sink and modern wall-mounted fittings.

Porcher's Metallizato above-counter basin marries copper and glass by fusing the metal between layers of iridescent glass for an extraordinary result.

SYNTHETICS, LAMINATES, AND LINOLEUM

The resource market is filled with a vast number of synthetic materials, laminates, and linoleum options to meet your every practical and aesthetic need. To find what's right for you, visit showrooms, talk to a designer, and page through shelter magazines and books for ideas. It's always best, however, to see a sample in person as surfaces can look one way in a photo and another in person. Keep in mind that when it comes to bathrooms, the tactile feel of a material is as important as the appearance because you will be touching the surfaces as you use the room.

 Acrylic-based polymers such as Corian (which can be molded into any shape and is practically indestructible) have become standards for creating vanity countertops, bathtubs, shower stalls and trays, wall cladding, and integral or vessel sinks. These versatile materials are available in hundreds of colors and patterns. Panelite, a resilient, lightweight, semitransparent material with a polycarbonate core that looks something like honeycomb, is being used by architects to create luminous walls, shower doors, and furniture. New resin products such as Lumicor (created by sandwiching botanicals, metal meshes, and handmade papers between two panes of acrylic resin) offer an artful alternative to glass panels and can be cut, drilled, routed, bonded, sanded, and thermoformed. Environmentally friendly, recyclable, and solvent-free, Parapan is a tough, high-gloss panel developed by Röhm Plexiglas and can be used for creating cabinetry and vanities.

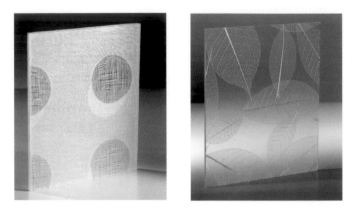

Lumicor panels are created by sandwiching textiles, etched metals, refined papers, and real botanicals between two thin sheets of acrylic resin. Applications include wall cladding, panels for light fixtures, vanity countertops, screens, and doors. At present, the company is working on a version that can be used for showers and sinks.

An all-organic laminate, Marmoleum is a jute-backed flooring from Forbo that's made of linseed oil, wood flour, and pine resins. Don't let its funky, modern looks fool you—this ecofriendly material (with anti-allergens to boot) has been around for a century. It's available in more than 150 colors in sheet form, tiles (backed with polyester), and special border designs.

For something fun on your walls: Flower Power from the Child's Play collection at Wilsonart is available in 3-, 4-, and 5' (0.9, 1.2, and 1.5 m) widths by 8-, 10-, and 12' (2.4, 3, and 3.7 m) lengths and can also be applied to doors, partitions, tub decks, vanity tops, and cabinetry.

La Chaise was designed by Charles and Ray Eames in 1948 for a Museum of Modern Art competition; Vitra began manufacturing it in small quantities in 1991.

The image of laminates has been revitalized with a plethora of new designs from classic companies such as Wilsonart that run the gamut of sophisticated metallics and stone look-alikes to vibrant, eye-catching colors and whimsical decorative patterns. Formica continues to develop new lines as well, including metallics, wood grains, and Etchings, a line that mimics the look of stone. Pirelli's studded-rubber floor tiles have long enjoyed widespread use in commercial venues, where they are appreciated for their resiliency, easy maintenance, and slip resistance. Recently they have made their way into the home, particularly in bathrooms and kitchens, where the Legos-like pattern of round, raised dots adds a playful and graphic presence.

In the arena of fixtures and furnishings, designer Hella Jongerious continues to fashion sinks of soft, foldable polyurethane for Droog Design while Agape has developed a folded PVC sink that's reminiscent of origami (see page 14). These pliable marvels make a fun, touchable addition to your bath. Jasper Morrison's Air Chair, a sleek, waterproof design made of fiber-glass-infused polypropylene, is intended for outdoor use but could be just as at home in a wet room or modern bath. In the same vein, Philippe Starck stretches boundaries once again with his Bubble Club sofa and armchair made of weatherproof, roto-molded polypropylene. And the molded fiberglass Eames La Chaise, designed by Charles and Ray Eames and manufactured by Vitra, is a classic free-form wonder that would make a stylish statement in a lofty bathroom with room for lounging.

FURNITURE

Bringing furniture into the bathroom makes it a warmer, more personal space. Upholstered chairs, chaises, and occasional tables all help to create an atmosphere that encourages lingering and relaxing even after cleaning up or getting ready is done. One recent trend has been converting antique tables, side boards, and dressers into vanities by adding above-counter vessels or built-in basins. It's not always practical to convert an antique, however, and it can be quite expensive, so another popular approach is to design and build a vanity that looks like an antique but has storage that's tailored to meet your personal needs. Furniture-like vanities are being produced in modern styles as well, in particular with sleek vessel sinks made of metal, glass, concrete, wood, and other unusual materials.

Although furniture can be incorporated into any size bathroom, a larger room has more space for extras such as seating and occasional tables to create a sitting area. Extras might also include a rack for magazines, a freestanding shelf for books, a rolling cart for a small television or stereo, or a cube that doubles as storage and seating. To bring in upholstered pieces, you'll want to be sure your bathroom is properly ventilated and that upholstered pieces are not exposed to water spray. Sticking to naturally absorbent fabrics such as canvas and terry cloth will help as well. Both can be used to make slipcovers to facilitate cleaning.

Built-in storage such as undersink cabinetry, walls of closets, and shelving are a luxurious element that can give the bathroom a streamlined appearance while providing plenty of space for keeping towels, toiletries, and other bath necessities. For people who just need a little extra storage but don't want to revamp their whole space, freestanding and wall-mounted options include repurposed curio cabinets, step ladders, storage lockers, and, of course, medicine cabinets.

Finally, designers are creating furniture suites intended for use in the bathroom (complete with coordinating accessories), such as those by Barbara Barry and Michael S. Smith for Kallista and Jean Marie Massaud for Dornbracht. With these stylish vanity and cabinetry suites available, it's now easier than ever to create a well-appointed bathroom that has all the amenities you need for it to double as a lavish dressing room or lounge.

Well-known designers such as Barbara Barry have created entire suites of furniture for the bath. The elegant mahogany dresser and vanity shown are from Barry's line for Kallista, which was inspired by 1930s modernism and can be coordinated with chairs, sofas, and tables from her line of furniture for Baker.

Made of aluminum plates and molded extruded tubes, the wall-mounted AERI-Aluminum storage unit (from the Whitehaus Collection) hugs the wall, giving it the look of a built-in cabinet. A full-length mirror helps with getting ready.

With hidden doors for storage, the Arcus Cabinet by Porcher is made of maple with a deep ebony stain and can be used with an above-counter basin for a dramatic addition to a contemporary bathroom. As shown here, the freeform shape of the mirror and the rounded metal basin sink provide a visual foil to the strong lines of the cabinet design.

Agape's Flat XL cabinet with a wenge-stained oak finish is a flexible design that comes with and without castors and fits neatly under a cantilevered counter or wall-mounted sink. It is shown here with a crystal glass countertop and the Spoon washbasin.

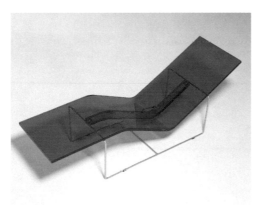

If you're worried about upholstery in the bathroom, consider the curvy Wave Chaise by Jean Marie Massaud, a stylish length of colorful translucent acrylic resin supported on a slim metal frame (from Dornbracht's Interiors collection).

Also from Dornbracht's Interiors collection, the Melt side table provides a handy place to hang your towel, leave a book, or set your glass and toothbrush.

DETAILS AND ADD-ONS

LIGHTING

Lighting is one of the most important aspects of bathroom design, but many people do not give it the thought it deserves. Design professionals recommend planning your lighting from the very beginning of your renovation, so that wiring can be installed and fixtures laid out in a way that works with the lighting plan. The two basic types of lighting you'll use are overhead and wall-mounted. Recessed and track lights are great in bathrooms because they add light but, as fixtures, are barely there, making for a clean, streamlined look. Ceiling-mounted fixtures such as pendants, chandeliers, and dome lights add more character but also take up more space. Wall-mounted sconces are perfect for adding task lighting and are often used on either side of a mirror or medicine cabinet. Available in virtually any style and metal finish, sconces make it possible to use lighting as a period detail or design accent that develops and enhances the style of your bathroom.

This sophisticated wall sconce from Urban Archaeology is inspired by a French design from the 1920s. The alabaster shade casts a soft light, making this a good choice for task lighting by the sink vanity.

An accessory/lighting fixture hybrid, Dieter Sieger's vibrant, light-infused designs for Dornbracht are available as cabinets, light boxes, shelves, and mirror frames.

WARMING DETAILS

Although your bathroom will require such basic necessities as decent heat (for colder climates), a cooling system (for warmer climates), and—this is very important—adequate ventilation, bathroom extras such as radiant floor heating, heat lamps, and towel warmers are the details that will add luxury and cozy comfort to turn your bathroom into a retreat.

ABOVE: Designed for heating ceramic- and stone-tile floors (and easy to add in a renovation), NUHEAT is like an electric "blanket" that's made to be installed between a subfloor and the tile. Although a builder or tile setter can install the mat, a certified electrician must complete the connection.

RIGHT: Heated towel warmers are becoming a popular feature in cold-climate bathrooms. The sinuous and linear designs add sculptural beauty to the bath while keeping towels toasty warm. Myson's Gavotte model goes well with a contemporary style and comes in three finishes.

MIRRORS

Mirrors add a sense of spaciousness to a bathroom as well as help you get ready for your day. Many design options are available, from flat, frameless panels to mirrors framed in beautiful wood or colorful acrylic to mirrored medicine cabinets. To break up a large expanse, you can float task lights (like sconces) in a mirror: The effect is magical and it puts your lighting right where you need it. Accessories such as a magnified mirror on an extending arm can make putting on makeup or shaving a little easier. But don't install too many mirrors: You don't want your bathroom to look like a fun house.

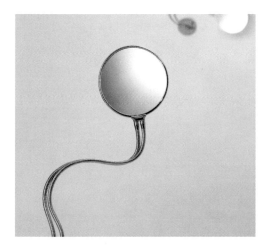

This wiry-armed mirror from Agape has two sides: one regular, the other magnified. The flexible support allows you to adjust it any which way, making shaving and makeup application a breeze.

This mirrored medicine cabinet (shown in polished nickel) from Urban Archaeology is called Lennox and can be gracefully incorporated into any decor. The interior holds four glass shelves.

A home gym can be the ultimate add-on to your bathroom. The amenities in this home gym in Amsterdam include an exercise bike, television, charming sloped ceilings, and a view.

THE ULTIMATE ADD-ONS

For many people, retreating into their home is the best way they know to relax and, subsequently, bathrooms are becoming increasingly multifunctional. Homeowners are installing deluxe extras such as dressing areas; spa features such as saunas, steam rooms, and massage chairs; personal gyms with free weights, treadmills, stair-climbing machines, and exercise mats; entertainment systems that include big-screen televisions and stereos; and seating areas for enjoying a cup of tea or reading a book.

SECTION TWO:
30 BATHROOM PROJECTS

Many people have wish lists of what they would like in an ideal bathroom: a whirlpool bathtub, radiant heat floors, a double-sink vanity, a frosted-glass shower stall. But how does one integrate an eclectic list of must-haves in a way that makes sense, so that the room is well appointed and doesn't look like either a jumble of mismatched fixtures or the spa at a gym? This is where design comes in. A successful bathroom design addresses both practical needs—Where should the shower go? Is there enough room for the toilet in that corner? What's the best sink option given the narrowness of that wall?—and aesthetic wishes—Are mosaic tiles right for this space? What kind of vessel sink would look best with this counter? Isn't that 1920s sconce just perfect? Creating a perfect of blend of usefulness and beauty, good design is particularly important in the bathroom because you want the space to feel welcoming and look good, but you also want to have a handy spot for shampoos or to be able to get into the bathtub easily and safely.

This section of the book includes 30 bathrooms that have successfully melded form and function, overcoming awkward layouts and structural limitations to create inspired and beautiful spaces that accommodate the needs of the homeowners while inviting them to spend time relaxing. Architects and designers share their thoughts on what makes the designs work, materials they chose to work with (and where they found them), how they resolved problems that cropped up along the way, and how their ideas might be adapted to fit into other homes.

The section has been divided in four chapters, according to the spatial parameters of the rooms: large and lofty spaces, long and narrow spaces, small spaces, and unusual layouts that defy categorization. Also included are floor plans and drawings to help paint a clearer picture of the room layouts and, in some cases, the custom-made fixtures created to accommodate the specific needs of the space. Finally, the In Focus sections explain how to plan a wet room, build an outdoor shower, create a memorable half-bath, and how technology can lead to the creation of smarter bathrooms.

From the beach cabana created by a London architect and his florist wife to the glass-walled bath designed by a Japanese architect to an open-it-up space tucked into the corner of a bedroom by a California architect, countless inspired ideas and practical solutions are contained in the following pages.

This stylish master bedroom and bath suite created by ColePrévost for a client in Washington, D.C., is a study in white with its translucent wall of acid-etched glass, sleek Philippe Starck tub, and classic white leather Le Corbusier chair.

LARGE AND LOFTY SPACES

While many people might consider a large and lofty master bath to be the ultimate luxury, the generous size can provide its own set of design challenges. Fixtures need to be properly scaled so that they don't look flimsy and, in colder climates, draftiness can be an issue. (Heat lamps and radiant heat floors are two solutions.) You want to organize the space so that fixtures relate to each other in a way that makes sense—for example, because the sink is generally the most-used fixture, placing it where it's easily accessed is important. You may want to have separate areas for bathing and showering, so that the tub can be open to the room or, even better, a view. Additionally, many people opt for a separate toilet compartment with a door, so that couples sharing a bathroom can still have some privacy when needed. And where room isn't an issue, a whirlpool bathtub or Japanese soaking tub is an indulgence that turns your bathroom into a spa.

Large spaces also lend themselves to the creation of a wet room, meaning the shower is open to the room, and wet and dry zones flow into each other seamlessly. Having enough room allows you to place more water-sensitive fixtures (such as a vanity or storage cabinet) out of range of the spray. Extra space also makes it possible to include upholstered furniture, such as a big comfy chair for reading or a chaise lounge for naps. Some people even install televisions and stereo systems, hiding them in built-in wall cabinetry for a more integrated look. Finally, there are the ultimate add-ons, such as a home gym—with mats, a treadmill, and stair-climbing machine—or a separate dressing area with a vanity that's just for makeup, jewelry, and adding those finishing touches before going out.

The London firm Amok designed this spa-like bathroom for clients in Brighton, UK. The space is divided into zones: The big soaking tub takes pride of place by the windows, a separate shower stall with glass panels lets light into the room, a toilet is tucked in the corner, and, cantilevered off the wall, a wooden vanity with double sinks makes it easy for a couple to share.

CALIFORNIA CONTEMPORARY

by Winston Brock Chappell

"This is a very contemporary residence on a hillside, but it feels more like a Zen temple on the mountainside," says architect Winston Chappell, of the house he designed and built for a client in Southern California. The bathroom, a 30' (9.1 m)-long expanse with views of a private wild canyon, is appropriately serene and loftlike and features plenty of creature comforts, such as a deep tub for soaking, double sinks, heat lamps, and separate shower and toilet niches.

The client's original home had been destroyed during an earthquake, so Chappell was building on a site that his client already knew well. The bathroom faces a nature preserve, and to bring the exterior landscape into the room, he installed a 10' (3 m)-wide steel-framed window. The window is like a giant picture wall filled with images of oak, pine, and eucalyptus trees. A black granite vanity is cantilevered off the framework of the steel window, which also provides the support for the two completely floating mirrors positioned over the twin stainless-steel sinks. "Most people don't notice the mirrors right away," he says. "They are startled to see themselves. It sets up a great play of perceptions."

The length of the room allowed the architect to divide it into zones. The sinks are immediately accessible on entry, as it is the first and last fixture used. To the right is the bath and to the left, the shower. "To most of my clients, these are activities they like to share with their partner," says Chappell. "Not necessarily doing them together, but it's okay if one is in the bath and the other comes in and sits in a chair to talk about their day." Out of sight, at the end of the room, is a private niche for the toilet with its own small window. The light from the many windows plays up the luxury of the simple materials that were used: glossy polished concrete for the floors; a rougher-textured poured-concrete on one wall; black granite for the vanity and tub; and reddish gold Douglas fir, which was used to frame the other windows and the sliding pocket doors that separate the bath from the bedroom. "Even though it's a very simple, very serene space," he says, "it's not cold at all."

OPPOSITE: A large steel-framed window with a cantilevered black granite vanity sets the tone for this bathroom, which is generously sized and appointed.

VANITY AND SINKS:

Cantilevered off the steel framework of the window wall is a 10' (3 m)-long vanity made from a slab of polished black granite. The twin under-mounted stainless-steel sinks (by Elkay) are fitted with polished chrome faucets from Chicago Faucets. The flat, wide wrist blades are the kind used in hospitals by surgeons; easy to maneuver, their stylish upward curves provide a visual lift that complements the high-arched faucet. The vanity has no cabinetry (there's a freestanding cherry cabinet for storage), so the plumbing pipes below the sinks are exposed; they snake toward the wall like metal sculptures.

POLISHED CONCRETE:

The concrete floor was ground and polished by a specialist for a smooth, silky surface. "The floor has a very luxurious feeling," says architect Winston Chappell. "There's absolutely no abrasiveness." Polished concrete is being used commercially and in homes as an alternative to such materials as marble, limestone, and tile. The high-gloss finish does not need waxing and can be stained for a variety of decorative effects. Additionally, found objects such as glass, bolts, or computer chips can be seeded into the mix and polished smooth.

The walls of the large room are broken up by the lines of windows in different sizes and shapes. Along with the window wall that dominates the space, there are smaller windows that are framed in Douglas fir. A clerestory window on the far end brings in light while offering privacy as that wall faces the garden. A square inset cranks open to let in fresh air and also makes the design less symmetrical. Another square window is located almost at floor level at the head of the tub. Bathers can soak in the deep tub and take in the lush, green view. Echoing the rectangular shape of the clerestory window but turned to create a vertical element is an 8" (20.3 cm)-deep niche; its presence warms the otherwise empty white wall and provides a vertical foil to the horizontal sweep of the long room.

For indulgent bathing, a deep Roman-style bathtub that's as long as the bathroom is wide occupies the far end of the room. It's made of the same black granite as the vanity, but has been honed to provide more grip for safety. The tub is undermounted, which allows the polished concrete floor to flow smoothly across the length of the room right up to where it drops off into the pitch-black granite pool. In the shower chamber (not shown), the same honed black

granite covers every surface. "With its clear, frameless shower doors," says Chappell, "the granite shower reads both as a reflection of the picture window and as a mysterious recess."

The need to build to code against earthquakes and fire drove decisions like putting in dual-glazed windows and heavily insulating the exterior cement plaster walls (against burning). One advantage to having enough scale to the house meant the architect was able to hide things. But the homeowner, an enthusiast of modernist architecture, embraced the idea of just letting the structure show when necessary. "If we needed to use a steel beam, she said, 'Go ahead,' " he says. This approach works well in a space that uses materials such as exposed concrete that are more traditionally at home in commercial buildings.

With its calming palette, generous proportions, and openness to the green view, the tranquil space seems like it has always been there. "We wanted this bathroom to be the essence of serenity," says Chappell, "but it took a lot of work to get it there."

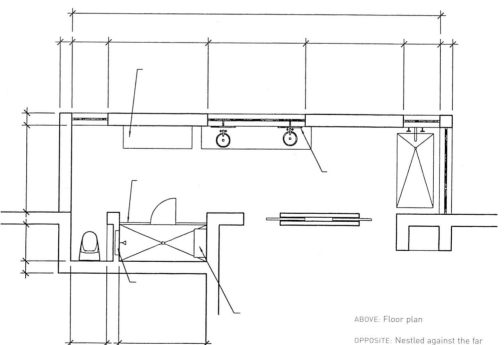

ABOVE: Floor plan

OPPOSITE: Nestled against the far wall is a Roman-style bathtub made of black granite. The honed surface of the stone allows for increased grip, and its matte appearance offers a pleasing contrast to the shiny, polished-chrome fittings.

BATHTUB:

The bathtub was custom made at the site using a combination of 12" (30.5 cm) square tiles and a ¾" (1.9 cm)-thick slab of honed black granite. "Basically, the construction is the same as a Roman tub with a removable water stopper," says Chappell. "We followed recommendations for 'Tile Tubs and Fountains' provided by the Tile Council of America. Strangely, Roman tubs are allowed to not have an overflow, which is a part of all manufactured bathtubs." Sculptural polished-chrome fittings from Dornbracht pop out against the black granite edging that surrounds the tub.

WINDOWS:

The far end of the bathroom is served by two windows. A clerestory window preserves privacy while letting in light and glimpses of the sky. The other is a small square placed at the head of the tub, so that bathers can enjoy the view while steeping and, when the window is open, a refreshing breeze. "By placing windows at the ceiling and at the floor," says the architect, "you get surprising views of things. Again, it's this notion of changing your perceptions, of keeping your home surprising."

DOUGLAS FIR:

Sanded and stained to a furniture-grade quality, this highly workable wood was used in several places: to frame the windows by the tub, to build a niche nearby for flowers, and to make the sliding pocket doors (which are inset with opaque laminated-glass panels). The reddish gold of the wood offers a warm, appealing contrast to the cool expanses of the concrete floor and black granite vanity and tub.

IN FOCUS:

PLANNING A WET ROOM

"You can put a wet room in any space," explains architect Winston Chappell. "You just want to keep the air moving and make sure the water doesn't hit something it can damage. With a good showerhead, you'll feel like you're in Costa Rica in the rain forest."

A wet room is a fun way to update a bathroom, but it might not be the right choice for everyone. "Most people move into environments that they know or have to accept, like a dorm room or an apartment," says Chappell. "For a lot of people, doing a bathroom, or sometimes a whole house, is the first time they've had to make every decision themselves." He suggests really thinking about how you'll use the space and carefully considering which design choices go with your lifestyle. So while a wet room can be installed almost anywhere, it's not going to be a good option for someone who likes to feel cocooned while bathing or the person who worries about getting the floor wet.

If you decide a wet room is for you, you'll need to keep in mind the following:

WATERPROOF FLOOR AND WALLS

Any number of techniques can be used to waterproof a floor, from laying down a rubber membrane to using waterproof concrete. The most commonly used waterproof membranes are multiple layers of roofing felt adhered with hot asphalt (known as "hot mopping") or PVC latex and other plastic membranes. If you plan to tile the floor, use small tiles (the grout lines increase traction) or ones that have a honed, nonslip surface. Slanting the floor slightly will direct water flow toward the shower drains. Treat the walls like they are part of the shower and cover them in a water-friendly material such as tile or stone.

DOUBLE YOUR DRAINS

"Always put two drains in the floor," says Chappell. This prevents flooding if one drain gets covered by a wet hand towel and also allows the floor to dry more quickly, which is a good safeguard against slipping.

VENTILATION IS KEY

A wet room is by definition wet, so good cross-ventilation is important to let out steam and moisture. The wet room shown has a window as well as a sliding door that opens onto a deck. "You don't want it to be a room where mildew can develop," he says. "You have to double the mechanical ventilation."

CONSIDER THE ZONES

Define the space by how you will be using it to help decide where the various fixtures and cabinetry should go. Then calculate how far the water in the shower area is going to splash, and make sure that nothing that isn't waterproof is in harm's way. Says Chappell: "You typically want to leave a larger showering area— about 8' [2.4 m] long by 6' [1.8 m] wide."

CHOOSE WATER-FRIENDLY MATERIALS

Although pretty much out of range of the shower, the walnut cabinet in the bathroom shown was still sealed with a two-part marine epoxy and given a limestone top, which is impervious to wetness. The little bench is made of teak, a hardwood known for its wet-weather durability and popularly used on boats and to make outdoor furniture.

PROTECT THE LIGHTING

In a wet room, the lighting has to be protected. "You can get enough steam in a room to shatter an unprotected bulb," explains the architect, "so you have to use light fixtures suitable for wet environment. Specialty lighting is readily available. The bulbs are typically covered with tempered glass or plastic— anything that's shatter resistant."

The walls and floors of this wet room shower look like polished concrete but are actually steel-troweled stucco with an added sealer. It feels like Venetian plaster to the touch, but the high-gloss finish gives the whole room a lush feeling that's just right for indulging in long, steamy showers.

INDUSTRIAL STRENGTH

by Archisis

Holger Schubert, the architect and owner of this expansive, state-of-the-art bath, was inspired in his design by traditional Japanese bathrooms. Having lived and worked in Japan, Schubert learned to appreciate the idea of separating the bath into three areas: one for the toilet, one for washing, and a third for bathing. "It's very common in Japanese bathrooms for the shower and bath to be self-contained," he explains, "so that once you close the door, everything can get wet."

Schubert re-created this concept of a wet area when designing his own home in Venice, California. Now an architect at Archisis, Inc., in Los Angeles, Schubert used the renovation of his own residence as a kind of working experiment for his conceptual plans. Devoting the entire first floor to the master suite, he carefully carved out sections of the master bath and dressing areas to accommodate every wish and practical need that he and his wife could imagine—right down to the space designated for mounting the couple's electric toothbrushes.

Carefully orienting the entire 12' (3.7 m) square room toward the exterior wall, which has sliding-glass doors that lead to a garden land-scaped with crushed granite and a wall of bamboo, Schubert designed the space so that

even the bathing area, when closed off, enjoys natural light and a view. He divided the area with a sliding curtain hung from a recessed ceiling track; the curtain extends the length of the room to entirely close off the shower wall and bathtub. When the curtain is pushed aside, the space is a lofty box with nothing above waist height to obstruct the view to the garden. The toilet room, a small space off of the washing-up area that can be enclosed with a sliding translucent door, is situated just inside the entrance hall and is entirely separate from the larger box of the space.

Using select materials and colors, Schubert wanted the entire house to feel cohesive and flow seamlessly from room to room. "I tried to limit the palette of materials to the absolute minimum and tried to keep it in the same hue," he says. "Throughout the downstairs level, the flooring is Spanish limestone (even in the closets) and there is only one step, which occurs when you enter the shower/tub area." The bath-tub and mid-height sink wall are both covered in slabs of the same limestone. Richly toned solid walnut appears repeatedly, as do plates of stainless steel that help to give the room its "concept design" aesthetic.

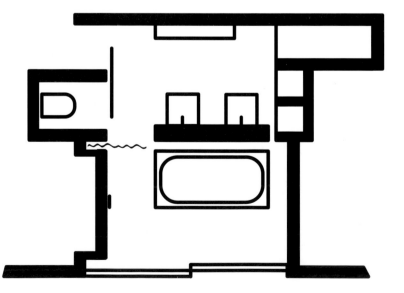

LEFT: Floor plan

OPPOSITE: This spacious master bath takes advantage of its open, airy floor plan. Architect Holger Schubert consolidated much of the traditional room dividers with built-in wall storage, a waist-high sink area in the middle of the room, and a bathing area that can be closed off with a sliding vinyl curtain.

SPANISH LIMESTONE:

Used throughout the first level of the house for the flooring, this pale stone feels soft to the touch. Schubert also chose it to clad the freestanding bathtub and the sink wall that serves as a mid-height room divider.

STAINLESS STEEL:

The stainless-steel shower wall is composed of nine square panels and is fitted with chrome temperature controls and a showerhead mounted flush with the ceiling. "This wall faces east and the sun shines right onto it, when it first rises," explains the architect. "It's also easy to dry and keep clean."

"I tried to achieve a very intimate space, but at the same time it had to be functional," explains Schubert. "I tried to eliminate things that are just standing around and address the storage problems that we had faced in our last bathroom." The paradigm of this decree is the electric panel he had built into the sink wall to hold his electric toothbrush and WaterPik. The minimalist pedestal sinks—each one simply a walnut column, inset with an angled steel tray rather than a basin—offer no storage space, but the architect made preemptive allowances by designing built-ins for everything that he and his wife use daily. Built-in soap dispensers and towel bars for each sink match the chrome Kroin fittings.

Orienting the sink wall toward the garden rather than setting it against an interior wall created the problem of where to put a vanity mirror. Insistent that nothing obstruct the airiness of the open space, Schubert created a sliding mirror that hangs, like the vinyl shower curtain, from recessed ceiling hardware. It can slide in front of the sink area when needed and slide out of sight into a wall pocket when not. Designed to be as minimal as possible, the mirror is hung from a panel of glass and is only as wide as one of the sinks. "It's the most unobtrusive mirror you could have," he says. "It doesn't take up any space at all yet it's very functional and really all you need in terms of having a mirror in the bathroom."

Although minimal in its design, the dimensions of the tub were meant to be anything but discreet. The 6' (1.8 m) tub is a standard fiberglass readymade mold with Jacuzzi jets, but it has been set into a Spanish limestone apron that is approximately 4" (10.2 cm) longer on all four sides. The top of the tub is flush with the top of the limestone apron to create a seamless box that is reminiscent of Japanese soaking tub. Lights inset into the limestone surround the tub on all sides, so that the freestanding structure can be completely illuminated at night. With a vinyl curtain to close off the window wall and another to shut out the rest of the bathroom, the tub can provide all the light necessary for a soothing evening bath.

In his effort to create a seamless expanse of open bathing area, Schubert made the ceiling a primary focus. He designed a drop ceiling throughout the house that would not only hide recessed halogen light fixtures, speakers, and other utilities but would also make the space feel taller and more open. "When the ceiling does not touch the walls, the space feels taller," he explains. "Your eye perceives the wall as not stopping but continuing upward." As a bonus in the bathroom, the ceiling also conceals the door and window frames, the tracks for the curtain wall and sliding mirror and the plumbing for an 8" (20.3 cm)-diameter showerhead so that water falls directly from above. The result: one large and lofty bath that feels even larger and loftier than its dimensions claim.

LEFT: The one problem with having your bathroom designed as the prototype for your dreams? "Everything needs an owner's manual," says Schubert. Sinks are fitted with a steel tray so that water disappears and is caught and drained through a basin hidden in the walnut column.

OPPOSITE: The view toward the water closet shows the minimalist door—simply a panel of laminated translucent glass that fits either the exact dimensions of the WC doorway or slides to the right and closes off the entire bathroom. A cutout serves the purpose of a door handle.

SINKS:

A minimalist creation by Holger Schubert, these rectangular columns are made of 1½" (3.8 cm) solid walnut outfitted with a stainless-steel tray that guides the water down into a hidden basin where it continues to drain. The stainless-steel plate where the Kroin faucet is mounted also serves as the charging base for electric toothbrushes.

SEPARATE BATHING AREA:

The stainless-steel shower wall and bathtub area can be sectioned off by dragging a vinyl curtain along a recessed ceiling track. Once closed off, the entire area can get wet, though the stainless steel and limestone usually dry very quickly.

WATER CLOSET:

A small room off the main space, the toilet chamber can be closed off with a sliding door of translucent laminated glass. The same door can close off the entire bathroom by simply sliding the glass to the right.

WEST COAST ZEN

by William Hefner Architecture and Interiors

"The idea of this bathroom was really very simple," says architect William Hefner. "The house it's in is on a hillside in Beverly Hills, and the room has a fabulous view of the city. We wanted to take advantage of that."

Because privacy was not an issue—the house is high on a hill and neighbors are far below it—Hefner placed the tub right in front of a large picture window. He chose a 3' (0.9 m)-deep Japanese soaking tub because its size makes it possible to see over the windowsill. A bench in the tub provides a place to sit and steep while taking in the expansive view. The tub's size made it awkward to get into, so to create a more graceful entry, the architect added a step. Both step and tub surround are clad in a cool gray limestone, with a honed surface that is subtle and sophisticated and also provides grip for safety. The dark stone blocks give the bath a visual heft and importance, making it a stunning focal point for the room, while the neutral material doesn't compete with what's outside the window.

Because the master bathroom was part of a new house design, Hefner had plenty of room to work with to create it. The homeowners knew they wanted the space to be symmetrical, and this idea is played out in the twin vanities placed on either side of a shared dressing room. Additionally, the husband is Asian American and had expressed a desire for the room to have an Eastern feel, which is reflected in the serene color palette and choice of materials. The warm, golden tones of the quarter-sawn maple cabinetry contrasts with the cooler tones of the frosted-glass privacy panel (for the toilet) and the honed-limestone floor tiles, countertops, and tub surround to create a sense of balance.

The only real drawback to a lofty room is the potential for drafts, so the architect installed heat lamps outside the shower area (not shown) to keep bathers warm as they dry off. The loftlike nature of the space had its advantages, however, as it allowed him to create large elements such as the tub and maple storage cabinet. By keeping the design simple and limiting the palette of each to a single color, he was able to give these utilitarian pieces a sculptural presence and draw attention to the beauty of the materials.

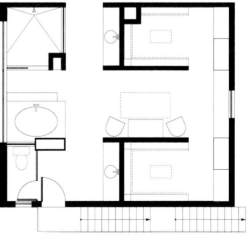

ABOVE: Floor plan.

LEFT: The twin custom maple-and-limestone vanities (only one is shown) feature white undermounted Ovalyn sinks by American Standard and 2020 chrome faucets by Newport Brass. Medicine cabinets are hidden behind the maple-framed mirrors on the side walls. The square drawer pulls are made of polished chrome.

MATERIALS:

Quarter-sawn maple was used to custom-build matching vanities and the high storage unit for towels. The floor and walls are tiled with Porto Beige limestone squares, while a honed slab of deep green limestone called Monte Verde tops each vanity. The tiles and slabs are all from Walker Zanger.

JAPANESE SOAKING TUB:

The white acrylic Fuji tub is made by Hydro Systems. Its deep design incorporates a bench for bathers to sit on while soaking, and a nonskid bottom provides safety. Available options include an in-line heater; swirling, rotating, or jumbo jets; low-voltage mood lights; a fiber-optic lighting system; an air-injection system; microban antibacterial protection; and grab bars.

ABOVE: In this master bathroom, bathing takes place right in the window; because the view is open but private, curtains or blinds are superfluous. Leaving off the window treatments also enhances the uncluttered, spare feeling of the room making it an appropriate choice for the distilled style.

LONDON BATH CABANA

by Peter Romaniuk and Paula Pryke

When London florist Paula Pryke was ready to expand her successful business, her husband, architect Peter Romaniuk, who had been planning to design a new home for the couple, took the opportunity to create the ultimate live/work space: 2,000-sq-ft (185.8 sq m) of living space above a 2,000-sq-ft (185.8 sq m) floral studio. Sandwiched between two Victorian warehouses, the new home is decidedly modern. "Peter had been inspired by the 1950s California Case Study houses," explains Pryke, "and so wanted to a create modern steel-framed house. In the '70s, there was a 'high-tech' movement in Britain and America, which used industrial components. These features are expressed within the building."

To maximize his budget, Romaniuk set out to create "the biggest envelope that would enclose the space at the most economic rate," says his wife. "The Case Study houses were also very cost-effective, simple structures." Once the box form of the house was defined, the architect set about forming a few specific internal spaces on the residential floors using lightweight partitions. The result is a light-filled, open-plan home that exactly fits the couple's needs and lifestyle.

The master bathroom is a lofty space with 9' (2.7 m) ceilings; large, round skylights; and a floor covered with white, studded-rubber tiles that are reminicent of building blocks. Within this industrial-style shell are inserted blue-and-white-striped canvas curtains that separate the space into zones, adding privacy and a playful beach-cabana feeling. "A degree of separation, privacy, and definition was called for," explains Pryke, "but the overriding idea was to contain the shower, the bath, and the dressing area each under its own circular roof light." The round, white-rimmed skylights float in the ceiling above the different fixtures, emphasizing the horizontal flow of the space. In contrast, the stripes of the curtains rise vertically from the floor culminating in a pool of light.

SERIES 7 CHAIR:

With its five wheels and easy-to-clean wood surface, designer Arne Jacobsen's Series 7 swivel chair is a fresh, modernist companion for the dressing table. Designed in 1955, the form-molded, steam-bent chair with a tubular steel frame is produced by Fritz Hansen (www.fritzhansen.com).

DRESSING TABLE:

A curve of striped curtain defines the area set aside for her: an old-fashioned dressing table for putting on makeup and getting ready for the day with lots of storage for cosmetics, jewelry, and other necessities. Made of burr ash with an etched-glass top and stainless-steel legs, the vanity is a new design made for homeowner Paula Pryke by Nicholas Pryke (no relation), a London furniture designer. The mirrors were purchased at The Conran Shop.

Inside and out, the house is inspired by the idea of a transparent home, with lightweight construction, nonpermeable materials, and translucent skins. Centering the activity zones beneath the round skylights ensures plenty of daylight and creates the sense that each area is a stage, which highlights the ritual aspect of bathroom activities. The privacy-creating striped-canvas curtains are shaped like half-circles, echoing the rounded shape of the skylights and creating a sense of enclosure. The couple had small circular stainless-steel rods fabricated and slipped them into pockets at the top of the curtains. The rods are used as a support for hanging the curtains. To keep the fabric taut, they tensioned the curtains with rope that's secured at the bottom to the floor.

Near the head of the bathtub, a curvy sculptural piece holds the sink, a mirror, and a variety of accessories and also houses the plumbing for the sink and tub. Pryke refers to the structure as a totem. "It seemed fitting that the taps, mirror, soap dish, and toothbrush holder should all have a single, unifying expressive element," she says. Numerous metal pipes, stainless-steel bowls (the bowl-shaped sink and an actual mixing bowl that was repurposed), and a round mirror are creatively joined to be both functional and visually arresting. A second, smaller sink station is located at the dressing table (visible on the floor plan), so that two people can use the space together.

The dainty dressing table was designed by Nicholas Pryke, a London furniture maker, and is both practical and decorative. "He invited me to a private viewing, and I discussed my dressing table needs," explains the homeowner. "The top drawers are divided to hold all the things a girl needs: makeup on the left and cleansing on the right. The bottom one on the right contains a hairdryer and brushes and combs, while the one on the left is for jewels. It was great fun designing this with the designer." By working closely with the furniture maker, she was able to tailor the table to fit her needs exactly. Arne Jacobsen's Series 7 chair on casters provides comfortable seating that can be swiveled or rolled to other parts of the room, as needed. The lemony yellow color adds a touch of whimsy to the sophisticated space.

ABOVE: In the master bathroom, director's chairs slung with blue-and-white-striped canvas nestle against curtains of the same fabric and are evocative of a California cabana. Black-and-white photographs by London-based photographer Kevin Summers reference the homeowner's profession and her love of flowers.

LEFT: Floor plan

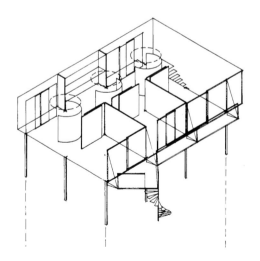

BATHTUB AND FITTINGS:

The sky-blue bathtub, from Aston-Matthews, is a reproduction cast-iron roll-top tub with decorative feet. In stark contrast to the Victorian-style tub, the faucet is a sleek, contemporary design in polished chrome from Vola. The one-handled mixer is a wall-mounted style that has been attached a metal pole—or totem—that holds up the sink (and contains the plumbing for both).

SINK AND ACCESSORIES:

At the head of the tub, the sink looks more like an abstract sculpture than something as utilitarian as a place to wash up. Assorted items were cobbled together to create it: a metal pole (which contains the plumbing); a large, round mirror with a swivel magnifier; a stainless-steel sink; polished-chrome Vola fittings; and a repurposed cocktail shaker and stainless-steel mixing bowl adapted to hold toiletries. The "arms" that curve out from the pole are actually stainless-steel, high-pressure hoses repurposed by the architect to act as plumbing pipes.

BALANCING ACT

by Cecconi Simone

When Elaine Cecconi, co-owner/founder with Anna Simone of Cecconi Simone—a Canadian firm known for its clean, elegant designs—talks about her work, she makes it all sound quite natural and effortless, a bit like the Zen philosophy that informs her company's aesthetic. But it doesn't take long to realize that achieving a look of casual grace requires a lot of planning, creativity, and attention to detail, with a fair amount of thinking outside the box thrown in for good measure.

Take the sinks in this luxurious master bathroom suite, created for a residence in Toronto's Forest Hill neighborhood. A custom design that is also a signature for the firm, these sculptural wonders are made of ¼" (0.6 cm)-thick Corian that has been illuminated from within. Flip a switch and the basin glows with a soft white light. They perch on top of chocolately wooden cabinets, the single unit containing the contrary forces of light and dark. "It's about creating harmony within a space," explains Cecconi, "the dark wood balanced with the Corian. One is old and familiar, and one is a new material. It's all about striking the balance."

To create the bathroom suite for their clients, Cecconi Simone first needed to rework the layout. The original bathroom was chopped up, so they combined the bedroom and bath, stealing some square footage from the old bedroom and connecting the two halves visually (and literally) though the installation of a two-sided gas fireplace. "We really wanted to integrate the bathroom as a part of the master suite," explains the designer. "That's why we used the two-sided fireplace. But we also wanted our clients to have privacy, so we added roller blinds." The blinds are concealed beneath the mantel, a smooth wooden beam that caps the tiled half-walls behind the sinks and runs the length of the wall, uniting the area visually by connecting the disparate elements.

OPPOSITE: With its shimmering basin sinks, rich wood cabinetry, and gas fireplace, this spa-like master bathroom indulges all the senses. Customizing their own designs allowed designers Elaine Cecconi and Anna Simone to integrate storage in invisible ways to create a harmonious space that is also highly functional.

SINKS AND FIXTURES:

The two large Corian basins are a design by Cecconi Simone called "Cecconi Simone II" (manufactured by RJW Enterprises). They are fitted with sleek, wall-mounted faucets in polished chrome by Vola. The softly glowing sinks are lit from within and mounted on custom cabinetry that has been stained a rich brown for contrast.

FIREPLACE:

An ultimate luxury, the bathroom and master bedroom share a two-sided fireplace from Majestic Fireplace. The gas fixture turns on and off with a switch for easily created ambiance that requires no fussing with logs and matches. For complete privacy, a woven fiberglass shade (made by Thermoveil Shadecloth from the 1000 Series) can be unrolled from beneath the dark wooden mantel.

HIDDEN STORAGE:

Every opportunity for storage has been cleverly maximized by the designers: They created spacious cabinets behind the large mirrors, complete with shelving that slides out to the side with ample room for storing personal items. Even the steps up to the bathtub (next page) have drawers tucked beneath them to provide a handy place for towels.

Although the bathroom is meant to be luxurious and spa-like, the designers didn't neglect practicalities such as storage. To maintain the clean lines of the design, however, they hid it within custom fixtures, taking advantage of any place that could offer easy access and sufficient room. The tub is encased in travertine and set high enough from the ground to require steps; this provided an opportunity to tuck drawers underneath the stairs. "We tried to take the basic elements that were necessary and make more out of them, enhancing them with storage," explains Cecconi. Additionally, there's storage in the sink cabinetry and behind the mirrors.

To unify the space, the design team carefully chose a few materials and then used them in several places, varying proportions to create a different look. The Autunno limestone that covers the floor in 18" (45.7 cm) square tiles also covers the walls but as 1" (2.5 cm) square mosaics. This is true for the main bath area as well as the shower stall and toilet niche (shown on the floor plan). "There's uniformity in the overall appearance but interest through the tile

patterns," Cecconi says. The designers also used the same dark-stained hardwood for all of the custom cabinetry and for the mantelpiece beam that runs horizontally across one wall. In this way, there is no demarcation of the room's furnishings and its architecture, but rather the two elements are connected and the transition between them is seamless.

The pièce de résistance is a Plexiglas planter that flanks the tub and is filled with tall, slender stems of petrified yucca. Downlights add drama to the arrangement, bringing out the beauty of the yucca while casting dark shadows on the tile wall behind it. And while the bamboolike stems lend the space an Asian feel, filling the container with another material such as wheat, grass, or stones would give it a completely different character. "Bathrooms are becoming more like spas, and it's nice to have your other senses stimulated as well," says Cecconi. "This is an element that can be changed seasonally or taken out completely. It adds to the space, creating an oasis."

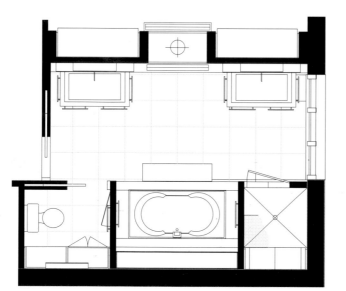

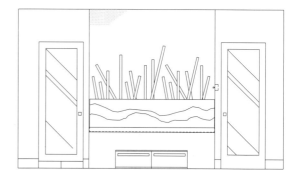

FROM LEFT: Floor plan, interior elevation

OPPOSITE: A seasonal element such as the planter brings change to an environment, giving it a lift and making the room fresh again. The steps leading to the tub make entry easier and safer, provide storage for towels, and heighten the drama by creating a special approach.

BATHTUB NICHE:

The snow-white, jetted-air tub from Ultrabath is surrounded by decking and a threshold made of antique-white crosscut travertine from Stone Tile. The deck-mounted faucet has a double-swivel spout and a hand-held shower set, all in a polished-chrome finish. To keep towels handy, slim stainless-steel towel bars by Hafele were trimmed to a smaller size and hung at each end of the tub.

PLANTER AND SPOT LIGHTING:

Creating drama in the bath niche is a stunning arrangement of petrified yucca of various heights and diameters that have been firmly inserted into layers of sand and pebbles inside a Plexiglas container. Recessed downlighting from Eurolite draws the eye to the arrangement. The container can be emptied and refilled with other natural materials in a seasonal rotation or simply removed.

MATERIAL PERFECTION

by JS Creations

"The space was nice to start with, but it had zero charm," says Jack Snyder, principal architect for JS Creations and the designer of this master bathroom renovation on Long Island, New York. "The existing bath had been redone in the '80s, with ceramic tiles and options that were luxurious at that time but felt dated by today's standards. The plan was to soften up the atmosphere and open up the room to the wooded area just outside."

By gutting the space, adding two skylights, and "opening up" the exterior wall with the addition of five new windows that looked out to a bamboo garden, the architect did just that. He then chose warm but modern materials and designed the fixtures with a similar aesthetic for an overall space inspired by industrial design yet customized for luxury comfort. And while "comfort" to an architect with modern sensibilities frequently overshadows the practical needs that will ensure a homeowner's everyday comfort, Snyder was careful to adjust each of his creative concepts according to the homeowner's needs.

"My biggest wish was for a wall of windows to flood the space with light," Snyder says, "but the homeowner was concerned about privacy. What we did was create a sandblasted middle section in the shower area, and then we extended that idea with window treatments along the tub wall." The result is a horizontal stripe of privacy that extends across the entire wall of windows but sacrifices almost no light or airiness. With frosted glass obscuring the view into the shower area and a pleated shade that can be drawn from either the top or the bottom, the window treatments are subtly integrated into the architecture to please both architect and client.

In another collaboration, the 6' (1.8 m)-long trough sink in a combination of limestone and stainless steel was designed to float on the wall. To soften the effect and create storage according to the homeowner's request, Snyder wrapped the vanity in honey-toned Anigré maple drawers with dividers of brushed metal that serve as drawer pulls. The original design idea is still there—an industrial metal trough set in a limestone countertop—and by raising the entire streamlined unit up onto skinny stainless-steel legs, it feels almost as though it's floating, despite the added heft of the much-needed cabinets.

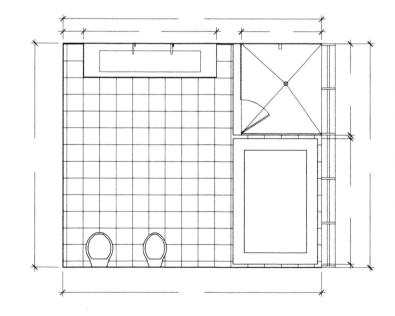

LEFT: Floor plan

ABOVE: A sleek, chrome, wall-mounted faucet from Kroin with a single-handled mixer helps to keep the stainless-steel trough sink free and clear of clutter. An adjustable limestone section that can slide along the trough divides the sink area and provides added storage.

FERRING STRIPS:

Strips of maple—each one finely sanded and sealed—were attached to the wall with carpenter nails in alternating directions to create a band around the room. "It helped to focus the eye when we hung them this way," explains architect Jack Snyder. "If they were all horizontal, it would look like some kind of racing band. If they were all vertical, you'd feel lost."

ANIGRÉ MAPLE VANITY:

For storage, a cabinet clad in warm-toned wood was installed below the counter. For even more storage, two medicine cabinets flank the center mirror.

TROUGH SINK:

The 6' (1.8 m)-long stainless-steel trough sink is fitted with two wall-mounted faucets from Kroin. Sunk into a 7' (2.1 m)-long limestone counter, the basin extends nearly the length of the vanity but can be separated with a sliding limestone shelf to divide the sink and add extra storage.

ABOVE: At 7' (2.1 m) long, the vanity belies its heft with skinny stainless-steel legs that raise it up off the ground and make it feel as though it's floating on the wall. Additionally, the use of contrasting materials adds visual interest to the large unit while maintaining a sense of uniformity with long, horizontal lines.

With plain white walls and standard porcelain fixtures, the original master bathroom was almost too big and lofty. "There was nothing for your eyes to focus on," says Snyder. "It felt kind of cold and hard." To counter the expansive nature of the space, he designed large, free-standing fixtures in both warm and cool tones that would feel modern and industrial while creating a comforting atmosphere.

The current focal point is the 6' (1.8 m) brushed-stainless-steel soaking tub designed by Snyder to complement the sharp, geometric angles found throughout the house. Knowing that he wanted a stainless-steel tub designed with mostly 90-degree angles, he made the edges wide enough to double as storage: 4" (10.1 cm) on the longer sides and 8" (20.3 cm) on either end. The inside of the tub is angled for comfort while soaking and has been outfitted with not only Jacuzzi jets but also a special rubber membrane on the underside to quiet the tinny echo created by water rushing in from the Kroin tub filler.

Using a limited palette of colors and textures, the architect chose materials with chameleon-like qualities to keep the space interesting. At different times of day, the slate chosen for the radiant heated flooring appears either powdery blue, blue-green, or sage. The brushed stainless steel was chosen for the sink, soaking tub, and shower floor because of its soft yet cool look and because the matte surface is easier to keep clean than a shiny one. Set against the limestone counter and slate flooring, the steel would have seemed cold without the presence of the warm wood elements on the walls and in the vanity.

The best and last obstacle-turned-design coup occurred when Synder was completing the wall finish. He knew he wanted opposing textures on the wall to complement the opposing tones of the steel against maple, but he didn't like the way his original idea was turning out. "We were going to trowel the plaster with a scoring trowel so that one section had the horizontal grooves and the next had vertical grooves," he explains, "but I didn't like the way it was coming out. The next idea was to do a flat finish alternating with a glossy finish, but then we had all these leftover ferring strips, which we were using to level the floor. Once we put them on the wall, we realized we could do the same thing by lining them up in alternating patterns."

At 15 x 25' (4.6 x 7.6 m), the high-ceilinged room could easily feel cavernous and cold, but a broad stripe helps to anchor the space. With the stripe on the windows lining up with the alternating wood strips, the focus is brought down to eye level. "There's a very soothing, calming quality to it," says Snyder, "not only because it's a repetitive pattern but also because it brings in some of the boundaries."

LEFT: A glass-enclosed corner shower incorporates all the elements of the master bathroom. The brushed-stainless-steel floor tray and ceiling complement the nearby soaking tub; the limestone walls match the adjacent vanity; and the large windows are fitted with sections of sandblasted glass for privacy.

OPPOSITE: An angular soaking tub in brushed stainless steel is the focal point of the room, particularly when complemented with a curvaceous bent-plywood stool. With a sharp, sculptural presence and backed by a trio of windows, the tub, designed by Snyder, appears more like artwork than a standard fixture.

**CLEAR GLASS AND
SANDBLASTED GLASS:**

Panes can be customized with
sandblasting or etching on
specific portions of the glass to
combine different opacities.
The lower two-thirds of the glass
in the shower was treated to
create privacy without sacrificing light.

SLATE FLOORS:

Using a natural stone such as
this pale blue slate, which
subtly changes color according
to the lighting, can be difficult
for builders because each piece
is not a standard size. "Not
only was each square a
different shape, they were all
different widths," says Snyder.
"We had to pour 3" [7.6 cm]
of mud so we could get
this floor to level correctly."

BRUSHED STAINLESS STEEL:

Snyder chose brushed stainless
steel rather than a shinier
version because it masks fingerprints and scratches. It is also
less slippery when wet—a good
point of consideration for
shower floors and bathtubs.

511 HOUSE

by Kanner Architects

A study in blue and white, the master bathroom in 511 House has a light and airy ambiance that was inspired by the nearby Pacific Ocean. Acting as both architect and client, Stephen Kanner relied on creative design to bring life to such commonplace materials as plywood, laminate, and corrugated fiberglass.

When designing his Pacific Palisades home, architect Stephen Kanner didn't have to look farther than his own neighborhood for inspiration. Not only is the oceanside location stunning, but the area is also filled with iconic houses built by Richard Neutra, Eero Saarinen, and Charles and Ray Eames. Kanner's own house is an elegant modernist design with an open plan, high ceilings, and numerous glass curtain walls. "The house is very close to the ocean, so I wanted to pick up a nautical theme and make it light and breezy. There's a tremendous amount of glass in the house," he says. "There are also a number of Case Study houses around the area, and the house picks up on and pays homage to those."

In the master bathroom, the palette is an aquatic blue and white, and the layout includes a ceiling that rises to 14' (4.3 m) at one end and a glass curtain wall at the other. The other exterior wall is closed off for privacy and is punctuated by the round windows that are a kind of signature for Kanner. As a whole, however, the house marks a stylistic departure for the architect, a self-proclaimed "Pop Modernist" whose earlier work is characterized by blocks of rich colors, strong geometries, and an enthusiastic use of round windows. (One famous example of his style is the prize-winning In-N-Out Burger.) "But now our architecture is much more minimalist," he says. "It's less Pop-y, with no round windows."

For materials, Kanner stuck to simple and affordable but made things interesting by using them in innovative ways. Throughout the house, he installed partitions of, and lined walls with, a dynamic, swirling-grained plywood. The plywood paneling connects the rooms visually, creating an easy flow throughout the house, and in the master bath, it adds a warming counterpoint to the cool tones of white and blue. The blue mosaic wainscoting in the bathroom is made of an inexpensive glass tile from Ann Sacks that was also used on the house exterior (which is mostly covered in a scratch coat of white stucco) to create a seamless transition from outside to inside. The architect did indulge in the occasional splurge, investing in dazzling white statuary marble for the floors and tub decking.

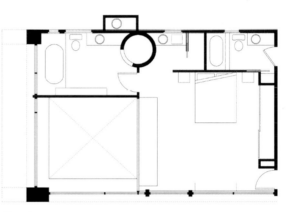

Floor plan

Custom mirrors float on the wall and echo the round shape of the windows, as do the small task lights over the vanity, the bowl-shaped stainless-steel sink, and the cylindrical shower stall. By repeating the round shape throughout the space in different sizes and incarnations, the architect unifies the miscellaneous elements of the bathroom.

TUB AND FITTINGS:

The elongated, undermounted white bathtub (model Alex 5 by Six-Eleven) is a standard width but 6' (1.8 m) long, allowing for someone quite tall to stretch out. It is fitted with a polished-chrome Dornbracht faucet. Elegant white statuary marble was used for the tub deck (as a slab) and on the floors. To add visual complexity, Kanner varied the size and placement of the material, cutting 18" (45.7 cm) square tiles in half and setting them on the floor in a running bond pattern. A roller shade attached to the windowsill can be pulled up to provide privacy without sacrificing light from the top half of the window.

The vanity—stylistically inspired by the work of Charles and Ray Eames—is a prime example of how creative design can work magic with inexpensive materials. The cabinet is built of medium-density fiberboard (MDF) and simply clear-sealed; the countertop is apple plywood that was laminated with white Formica. A bowl-shaped, stainless-steel sink is under-mounted into a raised-up countertop, so that when you stand in front of it, you can see the metal basin curve down into the gap. To make the sliding cabinet doors, Kanner chose white corrugated-fiberglass panels that express themselves as a series of undulating waves across the face of the sleek cabinetry. "They are really cheap," he enthuses, "but there's a lot of bang for the buck there."

The construction wasn't without its complications. For example, the diagonal support brace behind the glass window wall needed to go right where the tub was located. "The brace comes through a mullion in the clerestory window,"

explains the architect, "and we had to drill a hole in the tub deck marble. The trick was that the rod had to go through the hole before we completed the installation." He designed a round cylinder for the shower stall (the other side extends into the master bedroom) to pick up on the window shape and also "to make it easier to navigate around that corner of the room." To solve the problem of cladding it in plywood, he scored the back of the sheathing to allow it to curve around the form.

Although the bathroom's serene, clean-lined design is a more minimalist approach than Kanner's previous projects, it's not without a sense of playfulness. This is most apparent in the composition of circles that dance along the southern wall: a porthole window that spins open on its horizontal axis, its smaller companion floating like a bubble near the bathtub, and the vanity mirror that's an artful array of three intersecting circles.

VANITY AND SINK:

The vanity was custom built of MDF; instead of adding a veneer, the architect simply clear-sealed it. The countertop is apple plywood laminated with white Formica. White corrugated-fiberglass panels slide open to provide access to storage. The basic materials are made special through the exotic design. The faucets (see page 68) are from Chicago Faucets and feature the same wrist blades used for surgical sinks in hospitals. The flat, curved shape makes the handles easy to turn off and on, while also providing a sense of upward movement along the flat countertop expanse.

SHOWER STALL:

The cylindrical shape of the shower stall plays off of the round windows. Like various walls throughout the house, it's clad in CDX plywood. Here, it was scored on the back to curve it around the form. The interior has a lowered ceiling (for proportionality) and is tiled in the same 1" (2.5 cm) blue glass mosaic tile from Ann Sacks that's used on the bathroom walls. The threshhold is made of a slab of white statuary marble.

OPPOSITE: The plywood paneling that Kanner used to clad the outside of the shower stall reappears throughout the house as a theme, lining hallways, dividing rooms, and comprising cabinetry. The active grain patterns give it an organic, woody presence, making it an ideal foil for the many smooth, reflective surfaces in the bathroom—the glass mosaic tile, the Formica countertop, the mirrors, and the marble floor.

MODERN GEOMETRY

by Abramson Teiger Architects

"We've done a lot of bathrooms," says Trevor Abramson, a principal for Los Angeles–based Abramson Teiger Architects. "A bathroom should be a place of tranquility, a place to unwind. It should be very peaceful, with a Zen-like quality to it—like having your own spa at home. And the light that enters must be soft and soothing."

The architect's sentiment is reflected in this master bathroom for a family home in Los Angeles. Using a combination of materials that includes limestone, wood, granite, marble and sandblasted glass, the effect is naturally warm and soothing. Flooded with light from a wall of windows, the grid above the sink is constructed of honey-colored cherry and milky sandblasted glass. With flooring and countertops made from the softest gray limestone, the blend of these three colors and textures sets the tone for the entire space; it is a neutral, serene, tactile environment that seems to glow when the diffused sunlight hits the warm wood and glints off the chrome fittings.

Adding to this luminous atmosphere is a sense of order and calmness created by the repeating grid pattern along the window wall and the symmetrical under-cabinet storage. A continuation of a motif that is repeated through-out the house, this storage, constructed of tactile and warm-to-the-touch materials, elimi-nates the clutter and sterile aesthetic of many bathroom designs. Instead, it feels more like a study or meditation area.

"It made sense for planning purposes to put the sinks against that exterior wall," explains Abramson, "because I didn't want to sacrifice light by obstructing the only windows. So, we designed this grid that relates to the designs used throughout the house. The bottom two sections are sandblasted glass for privacy and the top section is clear glass. The mirrors are about 20" (51 cm) wide, which is all you really need. I don't like walls of mirrors—they can become very cold and sterile looking."

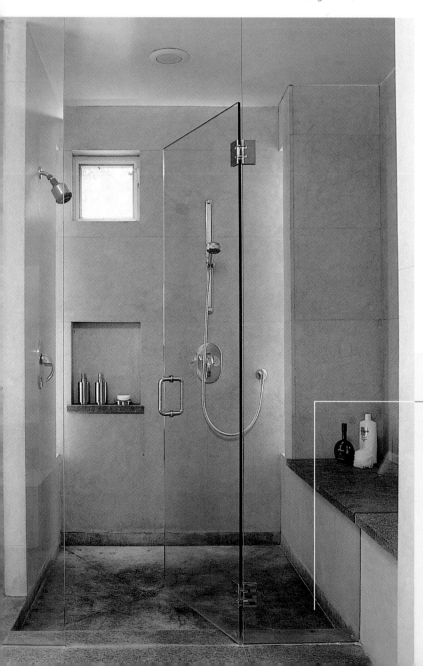

IMPERIAL RED FLANNEL GRANITE:

For the elevated shower floor and adjacent bench, the architect chose a mottled dark gray granite. One of the most readily available and durable materials, granite is a good choice for wet spaces and hot climates where cool floors underfoot are a welcome luxury.

LEFT: Seamlessly integrated into the wall, the rectangular niche provides a convenient spot for keeping soaps and shampoos at hand. Natural light filters through a small square window, which seems to hover in place.

OPPOSITE: An organized grid of windows supports two frameless mirrors and backs up a long counter of gray lime-stone. Maximum storage was carved out of the cabinetry to maintain order and peacefulness.

HIDDEN MEDICINE CABINET:

Hidden medicine chests keep the vanity area free from clutter. Disguised as a continuation of the window grid, these frosted glass panels open up to reveal deep storage cabinets. Located on both sides of the sink area, they operate by a touch lock.

SINKS AND VANITY:

An entirely customized wall was designed by the architect, Trevor Abramson, to contain double-sinks, maximum storage, hidden medicine cabinets, adjustable windows, and over-the-sink mirrors. With a limestone slab serving as the countertop, two sinks were dropped in a storage unit that was designed for keeping the entire space clutter-free.

FITTINGS:

The clean-lined chrome fittings—like the geometric faucets seen here—counter the lines and angles in the design with a sleek arc of a handle. Used throughout the bathroom, they are called Fino by Dornbracht.

The tranquility in this bathroom is due in large part to the blend of materials and the color scheme provided by this combination. But in addition to the soft gray limestone and warm wood tones, there are contrasting notes of hard stone, such as granite and marble, as well as strips of bright, pulsating color. As a way of keeping the bathroom from being too soothing—it must inspire at all times of the day including the morning when a jolt of energy is often needed—the architect included invigorating elements to create added interest for all the senses.

A cool slab of granite in mottled shades of dark gray with touches of carmine red is used for the elevated shower area that leads into an enclosed toilet room. Behind the tub, a glistening wall of Thassos White marble creates an icy backdrop for a hot bath. And then there are the touches of brilliant cobalt blue—in a painted stripe perpendicular to the soaking tub and another stripe of cobalt blue glass hung over white drywall, adjacent to the shower area. "I wanted to introduce color," says the architect, "and I knew I wanted this deep and vivid blue." According to color therapy, blue is said to have calming properties—it is supposed to slow the heart rate and make spaces feel cooler and more open. With its reference to the ocean and the sky, any shade of blue is a fitting choice for a sophisticated, spa-like bathroom, yet the pulsating shade used here acts as an invigorating burst of energy in an otherwise tranquil setting.

WHITE THASSOS MARBLE:

Excavated in Greece on the island of Thassos, this is the whitest marble in the world. It has a crystalline appearance that makes it glisten like a block of ice. A slab of this material was set behind the limestone bath to contrast the matte texture of that stone. In relation to the wall of wood paneling and the bold cobalt stripe, this combination sets up a repeated contrast of cool and warm.

PALE GRAY LIMESTONE:

Used for the floor, countertops, and tub surround, this pale shade of limestone is soothing and tactile. "Unlike other stones, it feels warm underfoot," says Abramson "and almost silky to the touch." It is ideal for use in relatively dry areas such as flooring and counters but is not the most durable option for extremely wet areas where water can cause pitting in the stone.

OPPOSITE: A whirlpool tub is encased in a soothing limestone surround and framed by a combination of Thassos White marble and vertical-grain Douglas fir with a surprising stripe of vivid cobalt blue paint.

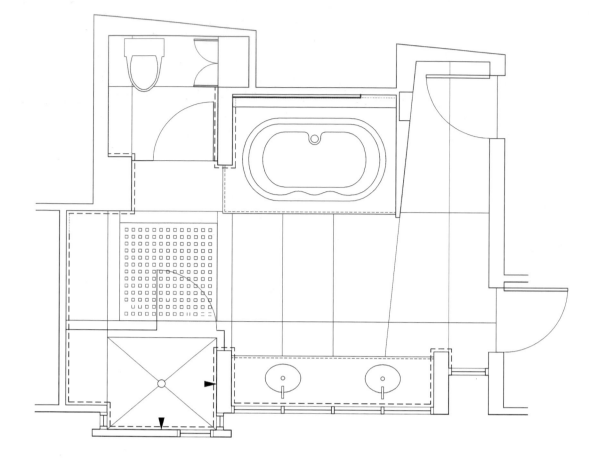

For further interest, Abramson added another wall of wood to create a hallway entrance to the bathroom. "I wanted to bring in more warmth," he explains. "There's nothing nicer than natural wood in a bathroom, especially in contrast to the cobalt blue and the icy marble next to it."

By dividing the wall of paneling horizontally, the vertical grain of the wood becomes an added feature and the grid motif is carried on. The constant repetition of geometric angles and grids in a contrasting blend of textures creates balance and order in this visually stunning master bath. It shows up again in the architect's signature bathmat—a grate of Douglas fir that is positioned outside of the shower.

The well-constructed layout offers spacious and separate areas for sink, bathtub, shower, and toilet. Organized like a series of small rooms

marked by their use of different materials but connected with a running theme of geometric order, the bathroom feels much larger than it actually is. Hidden storage—including a floor-to-ceiling closet in the toilet room and "invisible" medicine cabinets—eliminate the clutter of personal effects.

However, in addition to being serene and orderly, the bathroom was designed with function as the primary priority. Materials were chosen for areas where they would be the most practical: enduring granite for the shower floor, durable Douglas fir for the bathmat, limestone for tactile countertops and warm flooring, and Thassos marble for the tub backsplash.

ABOVE: Floor plan

OPPOSITE: The glass-enclosed shower opens onto a Douglas fir bathmat; designed by the architect, it's a grid that stands over a drain in lieu of a "soggy bathmat." The whole elevated area is set on a granite floor that is both cool and durable.

IN FOCUS:

A WOODEN BATHMAT

"The wood mat outside the shower has become a kind of signature of mine. I used that in a project ten years ago, and I've probably done it about ten times since then. I hate these shaggy rugs or mats that you see outside of showers all the time. The idea here is that you can drip-dry on the mat—there's a drain under it—and there's no puddle or wet rug to hang up," Trevor Abramson of Abramson Teiger Architects explains.

"Wood and water don't get on well without constant upkeep. [The mat] needs to be made of a dense wood. In this case, I used Douglas fir, but I have also used teak—which is the most durable—and iron wood. No matter which wood you use, it's a high-maintenance item, not for the slob, so to speak. You have to have a painter re-seal the grate about once a year."

HAMPTONS HIDEAWAY

by Betty Wasserman Art & Interiors

When art dealer and interior designer Betty Wasserman bought a 1936 cottage in Southampton, New York, it had all the charm of a salty seaside retreat. But before she and her family could enjoy the new summer getaway, it needed an entire overhaul to bring it into the 21st century and up to the luxury standards of a Long Island weekend home.

The three-bedroom house had never been renovated, so it still had its 1930s style and layout, with linoleum floors and vintage cabinets in a tiny kitchen. But the biggest drawback and near-deal-breaker was that there was only one bathroom, which was fitted with a tub. There was no shower and certainly no master bathroom. With the help of an architect friend, Glen Leitch, Wasserman decided to expand an upstairs closet into a 200 sq ft (18.6 sq m) master bath. "Glen suggested we convert the tiny upstairs closet into a bathroom," says Wasserman. "But I didn't want a tiny bathroom. I wanted a huge master bathroom. This is where I come to relax, so I wanted to be able to steam or luxuriate in a long, hot bath after I play tennis."

To create the space for Wasserman's dream bathroom, they punched through that closet and nearly doubled the size of the second-floor dormer with a new one placed directly over the front door, thus also redefining the entire facade of the house. She drew up some initial sketches and a wish list that included lots of counter-space, a freestanding two-person tub, and a steam shower. The team then worked to make it happen with new plumbing, luxury fixtures, retro-inspired accessories, and a few creative designs that Wasserman built for herself (and now sells through her website).

Sketch of the vanity

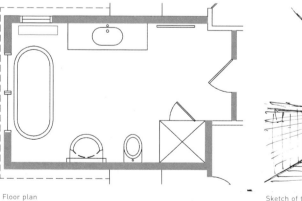

Floor plan

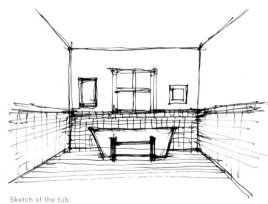

Sketch of the tub

OPPOSITE: Colorful accents add a dose of whimsy to this classic yet chic black-and-white bathroom designed by Betty Wasserman for her own weekend home in the Hamptons.

FLOORS:

"Unless you have really nice wood floors, it's hard to get an even, opaque finish using just a stain," says Wasserman, who ebonized (or blackened) the oak flooring throughout the house. Here, ¾" (1.9 cm) strip oak floors were installed and, using a combined process of dying, staining, and sealing, were colored a dark rich brown. For a simpler process, but less opaque finish, try a one-coat product like Dura-Seal's Penetrating Finish Stain in ebony.

BATHTUB:

A freestanding tub positioned under a window in a large, open bathroom easily becomes the focal point in the room. The Pier bathtub from Waterworks is an oversized, two-person soaking tub held in place by an ebonized-cherry and stainless-steel frame designed by Wasserman. The old-fashioned exposed tub filler, from Waterworks' Elsa collection, is a chrome reproduction of an antique design that complements the tub's modern style.

WINDOWS:

A nearly 6' (0.9 m)-wide opening was left for a new window when this bathroom was added onto the front of the 1930s cottage. Having salvaged the original casement windows during the renovation, the designer repurposed them (such as this large square window above the tub) throughout the newly renovated house.

Wasserman combined classic elements, in keeping with the building's original 1930s design, with modern pieces for a personalized, eclectic look. She added a classically inspired chrome shower attachment to a sleek, modern tub, creating an artful sculpture and an homage to a classic freestanding claw-foot tub. The bathtub looks streamlined in its black stand with stainless-steel accents and echoes a similar design in the single-basin vanity, a modern black cabinet paired with retro fittings. The duality of mixing old and new styles can be seen throughout the space and in many of Wasserman's other design projects.

By maintaining a strictly black-and-white palette in the building materials, the designer was able to create a cohesive and pulled-together atmosphere despite the mix of styles and periods. The floors were ebonized with a combined process of dying and staining for maximum opaqueness and the darkest finish. Wasserman then chose simple black-and-white ceramic tile that was ordered specifically to look like classic subway tiles. Shiny chrome accessories and fittings were coordinated with updated variations on traditional glass sconces in chrome and frosted glass.

The simple contrasting color scheme not only creates an overall sophistication and subtlety but also offers greater freedom for decorating. Colors and patterns can easily be added in splashes with towels, rugs, and accessories, depending on the homeowner's mood: bright shades for springtime, cool blues and greens for summer. Just as easily, she can revert to a classic look by replacing the linens with fluffy, hotel-style white Egyptian cotton.

With its full walk-in steam shower, two-person tub, generous vanity, and dressing table, this space is for pampering and getting ready. The designer wanted it to feel open and airy so that more than one person could enjoy the room at once. "It's nice to be able to hang out with friends while you're getting ready," she says. "Everyone always congregates in the bathroom, anyhow."

LEFT: The vanity is another of Wasserman's creations. It offers a glamorous spot to sit down and pamper yourself or simply read a book while you wait for the enormous tub to fill.

OPPOSITE: Mixing retro-style reproductions with sleek, customized designs resulted in a unique blend of styles and references that come together for a timeless, chic effect.

CABINETRY:

To double the size of a standard medicine cabinet yet still maintain the look of a large, seamless piece of glass, Wasserman designed a cabinet with a mirror that lifts up like a garage door. The design, called Sidney, is now sold on her website (www.Bettyhome.com) and can be ordered in custom sizes. The low white cabinet for holding spare towels and linens is a salvaged upper cabinet from the original kitchen. Wasserman saw it sitting on the floor during the renovation and cleaned it up and set it on four skinny chrome legs.

VANITY AND SINK:

"The key is to have a lot of storage space and a lot of counterspace," says Wasserman. When designing the spacious vanity for her bathroom, she lightened the appearance of the hefty piece by raising it up on chrome legs. The ebonized cherry cabinet provides plenty of surface area and storage room and, with its streamlined silver hardware, feels like an elegant piece of furniture rather than standard bathroom cabinetry.

SUBWAY TILES:

The designer special-ordered her tiles from Stone Source in black and white. They are 3 x 6" (7.6 x 15.2 cm) porcelain tiles, commonly referred to as subway tiles because they were used for the walls of New York's first subway stations. Once hard to find and even more difficult to replace, these tiles are becoming readily available. For a wide selection, check the manufacturer DalTile or Walker Zanger's Soho collection.

LONG AND NARROW SPACES

Inherited bathroom layouts can sometimes mean trying to turn a negative into a positive. One way to do this in a long and narrow bathroom is to emphasize the linear flow of the room to create a slender, elegant space. Lining all of the plumbing along one wall not only is a cost-effective way to install fixtures, it also creates a streamlined look and maximizes the room's open space by not cutting it up. Two popular approaches to layout are placing the tub/shower at the far end of the room or, if a room is wide enough, installing it along a wall lengthwise. Cantilevering a vanity off the wall makes the floor look larger, which in turn makes the room look larger. A wall-mounted toilet can do the same and has the additional advantage of being easy to clean.

The biggest challenge for a long, narrow bathroom, especially one with a single window at the end, is lighting. Doing away with window treatments or keeping them minimal (sheers or vertical blinds) opens up the room, and using white or light-reflective colors for tiles and paint creates the illusion of more space. Recessed lighting can light the interior without the need for bulky over-head fixtures, and task lights near the vanity can assist with grooming. Well-placed mirrors can also add light and a sense of spaciousness. For storage, consider floating shelves along a wall to emphasize the room's length or creating fully integrated, built-in storage for a stream-lined appearance. Finally, in-shower niches or shelving for storing toiletries helps keep clutter off of the countertops and tub decking.

By balancing matte and glossy surfaces and working within a white palette, the Canadian design firm Cecconi Simone created an open and refreshing space in which light plays over the marble surfaces, adding movement and life. Built-ins such as the cabinetry along the far wall and the twin vanities flanking the tub provide storage without adding bulk. Containers integrated into the marble counters make it possible to include an organic element, such as a seasonal display of flowers and plants.

PARIS IN NEW YORK

by Delson or Sherman Architects

DOORS:

All of the doors are custom made with solid teak rails and stiles. Ribbed glass panels are by Bendheim Glass; ceiling tracks are by Stanley; floor tracks and sheaves are by Hettich. The main access door is hung on three stylish industrial hinges. Fashioned after a design by Marcel Duchamp, this door latches in three positions to provide private or public access to the bathroom, allowing the family to tailor the space to fit their changing needs.

SHOWER:

The ceiling-mounted showerhead is the Etoile design by Waterworks in matte nickel. Fittings are also from Waterworks: the Elsa wall-valve trim and Elsa concealed thermostatic shower–valve trim, both in chrome. Delson or Sherman Architects customized drying rods for laundry from 1" (2.5 cm) stainless-steel pipes.

ABOVE: Floor-to-ceiling glass doors slide shut, turning the master bathroom into a long, slender hallway that connects the apartment and the master suite. With its white hexagonal tiles and high-end, modern fittings, the space is a stylish amalgam of old and new.

Inspiration comes in many shapes and sizes. In this instance, it was a door created by Marcel Duchamp, the French artist who so famously exhibited ready-mades as art. The door, used in his Paris apartment, was designed to latch in two positions to serve two doorways. Jeff Sherman, a principal at the Brooklyn-based firm of Delson or Sherman Architects, had seen one like it in the apartment of Duchamp's godson and adapted the idea for his clients, who needed a bathroom that could serve as a master bath, a laundry area, and also a half bath for dinner guests.

The apartment is located in a row house on New York City's Upper West Side and like many urban spaces, it has seen its share of renovations, including an extension out the back that resulted in a long, snaky apartment shape. The architects turned this extension into a master suite, but to win more space for the bathroom, they combined it with its hallway, creating a passage with multiple wet chambers. As you approach from the dining room, the first is a half bath with toilet and sink; the second, a tub and shower; and the last, a laundry room.

"The starting point was the problem of that long hallway," explains Sherman. "It had two tiny bathrooms with doors right next to each other—an awful layout—but we needed both a master bedroom and a powder room for guests. So the problem became the inspiration." By combining the two baths into one and opening up the claustrophobic spaces, the procession became much grander, and the area gracefully accommodates the family's need for public and private spaces.

And this is where the door comes in: Separating the master bedroom and bath suite from the rest of the apartment, the door latches in three positions. As shown (at left), it closes off the whole space for total privacy. It can also close off the half bath when it's in use or swing all the way over so the bathroom is open and accessible. "The door allows you to change the nature of the hallway," says the architect. "Closing off the master suite makes the hall part of a huge private bathroom. But for guests, you can leave the door open and close all the sliding doors. Then the hall becomes a vestibule for the guest WC, and the private family areas remain private."

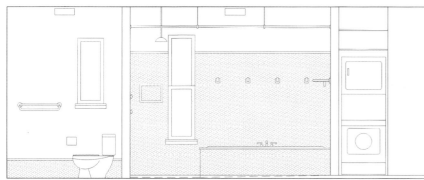

ABOVE: The open door gives public access to the streamlined bath as a hallway.

LEFT: Interior elevation

Instead of trying to disguise the skinny shape of the space, Sherman embraced it, turning a negative into a positive. "Often when people are faced with long, narrow spaces, they want to chop them into squarish rooms," he says. "But we've done just the opposite—slicing a long, narrow space into even skinnier strips." This theme is played out in a variety of details that also, not incidentally, serve specific client needs. One example is the slender metal bars in the shower area (see photo, previous page), which provide a place to dry wet clothes while also highlighting the room's elongated shape.

The awkward area was also made more fluid by smoothing out the walls. "Originally, the wall had a bunch of jogs," says the architect. "We angled the hallway slightly to streamline the whole thing." On the opposite side, they ran a long track of sliding doors, which when open erase the divisions between the room's dry and wet areas. Thus, this multifunctional space is not only public and private, but also wet and dry, a factor Sherman took into account when choosing materials. "The doors are all teak and ribbed glass, which is vaguely nautical and also weathers well when exposed to water," he says. "It's an amphibious space, and the materials needed to reflect that."

To blend with the apartment decor—the homeowners have an eclectic mix of old and new pieces—Sherman looked for materials that could be both. The hexagonal tiles are similar to those found in Manhattan's prewar apartments and provide a reference to that history. To make them contemporary, he played with the design and scale, arranging the gray detail tile in a more spaced-out pattern. Similarly, ribbed glass is usually found in older commercial spaces but is made new by its use in an original way. "The pairing of new and old materials creates a dynamic tension," says Sherman. "Like pairing foods that are sweet and salty."

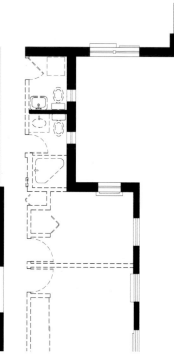
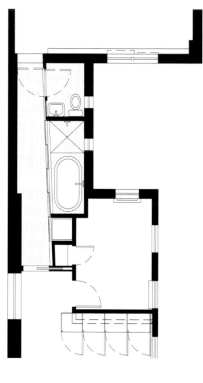

FROM LEFT: Floor plans, before and after

OPPOSITE: Tucking the tub behind doors makes for a cozy bathing experience. Choosing a neutral color such as white for installed materials and fixtures allows for maximum flexibility: Vivid towels, scented candles, and fancy soaps can all add mini jolts of color and will stand out against the white surfaces, while pure white towels and bath accessories add up to a classic look.

TUB AND FITTINGS:

The whirlpool tub is the Waterworks Classic Small Oval in white with matte nickel trim. Fittings are also by Waterworks, namely, a deck-mounted tub filler from the Elsa series in chrome.

TILES:

The floor and wall tiles are DalTile 1" (2.5 cm) hexagonal tiles with white grout. Sherman chose the shape to give the bathroom a slightly old-fashioned look to connect it to the prewar style of the town house. He gave it a contemporary spin, however, by adding a gray detail tile in a more spaced-out pattern.

TOWEL SHELF:

Located on the far wall, a polished chrome 20" (50.8 cm) towel shelf from Ginger's Hotelier collection adds a touch of luxury and a further nuance to the old-is-new theme of the bathroom.

SERENE IN GREEN

by The CALLA Companies

At 6' 2" (188 cm), British-born designer Andrew Lewis, principal of The CALLA Companies, is a tall man. So when it came to planning this bathroom, located in a brownstone in Boston's South End that he and his wife had bought and were renovating, one thing was certain: They were keeping the room's original 6' (1.8 m) cast-iron claw-foot tub. "It's long enough so I can really lay out in it," he says. "We wanted to keep it, but once the sink, tub, and toilet were in place, we wondered, 'Where would the shower go?'" Working around the spatial limits imposed by the tub's size combined with the long narrow shape of the room not only determined the room's layout but inspired the glass half-stall that is its focal point.

In order to keep plumbing costs down, Lewis ran all of the plumbing along one wall; and lack of room dictated that the shower would need to be located in the tub instead of separately. "We could have put in a shower curtain, but we're not really Victorian shower curtain people," he says. "We wanted to find a more interesting solution."

His original plan was to create a kind of glass shower stall with walls on the sides and front, but although he loved the concept, it wasn't really practical. "It looked cool on paper," he explains, "but if you want to bathe kids in there, you would have to open the door, and that's awkward." Because the bathroom would be for guests, he didn't want to limit the tub's accessibility.

To solve the problem of the missing front panel, which would have shielded the room from splashing water, he put a drain into the floor beneath the tub and pitched the floor to direct water toward it. For waterproofing, he installed a rubber membrane over the whole subfloor before pouring the concrete base and adding tile. To blend the style of the bathroom with that of the house, which still has all of its original wood moldings, he ran several rows of the floor tile as a molding along the bottoms of the walls, a subtle detail that gives the room a finished look.

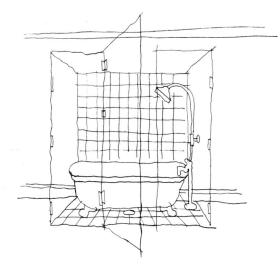 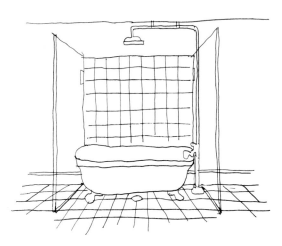

FROM LEFT: The original shower design and its revision.

OPPOSITE: Modern mosaic tiles and fixtures don't detract from the classic appeal of this charming bathroom located in a Boston brownstone, which still has its original window moldings and cast-iron tub. But the shower stall and high-end shower make it clear that we have definitely entered the 21st century.

ANTIQUE BATHTUB:

Before the antique cast-iron tub was reinstalled
in the bathroom, it had to be refinished. Designer
Andrew Lewis advises shopping around for
a refinisher and always trying to find a referral.
A properly refinished tub should last a long
time, whereas an incorrectly done tub can start
to chip in as little as three months.

EXPOSED SHOWER:

The Sunrise Specialty Company shower in
polished chrome and porcelain provides
a sculptural presence in the center of the room.
Water is accessible in three ways: A wide
showerhead overhead (attached to the ceiling
for support) allows it to cascade like rain;
a handheld showerhead assists in bathing small
children; and a faucet near the bottom of the
pole runs water into the tub for baths.

FRENCH TILES:

A 1" (2.5 cm) French ceramic tile, made by Emaux de Briare, was used in a green colorway on the floor and the shower wall. The mosaic pattern on the wall is a standard one provided by the company. The placement of the glass panels on either end of the tub was dictated by not only its width but by the amount of space needed to complete the tile pattern.

SINK AND FIXTURES:

The white pedestal sink and toilet are both by Kohler. A polished-chrome faucet with porcelain levers by American Standard was found at the Home Depot. It coordinates well with the style of the high-end showerhead but was much less expensive.

LIGHTING:

Contemporary chrome-and-glass sconces—a style called Top Wall by LBL Lighting—flank the mirrored medicine cabinet and provide task lighting for applying makeup, shaving, and washing up at the sink. The tub and shower area is illuminated with track lights.

ABOVE: Splurging on a shower can add a lot to a bathroom both aesthetically, when the fittings are especially beautiful, and practically. This shower works as an overhead, hand-held (great for bathing kids or just rinsing your feet), and tub faucet.

The tempered-glass panels on either side of the tub are held in place via polished chrome fittings attached to the walls and floor. Lewis had considered frosting the panels for privacy but ultimately decided he wanted the whole room to be visible when you entered, instead of having screened-out areas. "I'm glad I didn't do it," he says. "It would have been a mistake. The room is not really big enough to have the philosophy of it being revealed as you walk through it." The slight transparent presence of the panels does, however, define the bathing space. Additionally, a decorative backsplash made of colorful 1" (2.5 cm) ceramic tiles connects the two panels, creating a backdrop that is almost like a stage. "Because the space is defined, we needed to do something with that wall," he says. "But there could have been a hundred variations of tile there. We always wanted to frame the tub, and we thought it would be fun to have it look like a shower that just happens to have a big tub in the middle."

Another important element of the bathing area is the Sunrise showerhead, a beautiful polished-chrome and porcelain fixture that looks like a piece of sculpture. "We sort of splashed out on the shower," admits Lewis. "It has five or six taps and there are three different ways to

get water." Because the shower is so central in the room and so visible, the fittings have a particularly strong impact, so this was a good place to stretch the budget. By contrast, the fittings on the sink are "very standard," says the designer. "I went to the Home Depot and bought the cheapest ones that I felt worked in the space." A good strategy for maximizing a renovation budget is to freely combine higher-end items that have a special design with readily available ones.

To create visual interest on the wall opposite the tub, Lewis purchased four big polished-chrome coat hooks from Restoration Hardware and hung bath towels from them. The draped fabric softens the room and adds a sculptural element to the space. The hanging towels are grounded by the presence of a small velvet bench, conveniently placed so that bathers can sit down to dry themselves off. The wooden table with a drawer is part of the bench and provides storage for bathroom items.

With its palette of creamy white walls and sea-glass green tiles, the bathroom has an atmosphere that is aquatic and serene. Combined with the visual openness of the space, the result is a truly inviting oasis.

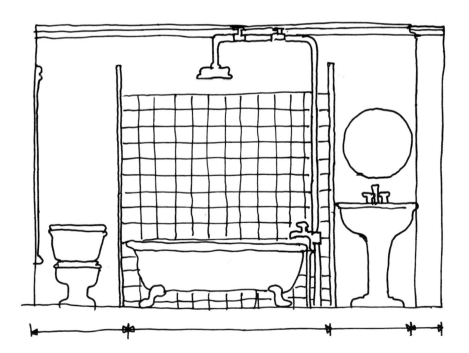

ABOVE: Interior elevation

BATHED IN LIGHT

by Henry Mitchell Interior Architecture

When it comes to design, sometimes it's the structural limitations of a project that end up inspiring an extraordinary result, as was the case for this light-filled shower located in the bathroom of a 12 ½' (3.8 m)-wide Brooklyn, New York, town house.

At just shy of half the width of the house, the bathroom has a long, skinny layout, which was complicated by the presence of a floor joist that limited the moving around of fixtures. "I had wanted the toilet further in the bathroom but couldn't do it because of the joist," explains interior architect Henry Mitchell, "so that dictated the arrangement of the bathroom and meant the shower had to go at the end. But that's how we got a really great shower." Additionally, because the homeowners had decided against a tub, extra room could be devoted to the shower as the primary bathing area. "We created a generous shower," he says. "Four people can actually fit into it comfortably."

Because the window was in the front of the building facing the street, he needed to find a solution that granted privacy but didn't block light or alter the look of the facade. His solution was to cover the floor-to-ceiling window with an opaque glass wall created by stacking three panes of acid-etched glass and framing them in ¾" (1.9 cm) metal mullions. Splitting the wall into three panels instead of one was more cost-effective and also made it possible to get the glass into the room through the house. "Two panes would also have worked," says Mitchell, "but that would have split the room visually. Using three felt the same as one." The addition of the brushed-aluminum framing was a purely aesthetic choice; it helps define the area and gives the wall an almost shoji-like presence.

To waterproof the shower area, the designer took up the hardwood floor, and then poured a layer of concrete before installing a lead pan. The presence of the floor joist meant he couldn't make the shower floor lower—his preferred method of handling drainage—so he built a lip threshold to keep water from flowing onto the rest of the floor. A tempered-glass panel helps keep the room dry while people are showering but lets light stream through and doesn't interfere with the open feel of the shower. Another option, which the homeowners ultimately decided against, would have been to create a wet room by leaving off the panel.

OPPOSITE: Doing away with a tub made it possible to create a generous shower with floor-to-ceiling mosaic tiles and two rainmaking showerheads. The acid-etched glass wall was installed to provide privacy, but the effect is pure magic: As the sun hits the window outside, the whole space is infused with light.

SHOWER AND FITTINGS:

The pair of wide, rainmaking showerheads (from Design Source in New York) creates a lush shower experience. A single thermostat mixer controls the temperature, but separate volume controls (by Grohe) assure that both showers don't automatically come on if just one person is bathing. A second drain accommodates the increase in water when both showers are in use.

After splurging on the high-end showerheads, the homeowners wanted to cut costs in other places. Mitchell was able to accommodate them with the double sinks, which he made from inexpensive Vietnamese lacquerware bowls found in a Manhattan store. He had his contractor drill holes in them and added drains purchased at a specialty store before mounting them on the vanity. "The idea came out of a sheer budgetary restraint," he says. "Sinks are expensive, so sometimes I'll use a salad bowl or mixing bowl to make one. Copper is more high maintenance, but some people don't mind that. You can get copper drains to use with a copper bowl."

The vanity itself is a sleek, modern piece that's cantilevered from the wall. "The contractor built it to my specifications," says the designer. "Cantilevering is not complicated to do. You approach it the same way you approach hanging kitchen cabinets, by attaching the piece to the studs to support it. You could also pick up the long braces that go on the back of wall cabinets at a Home Depot and hang it from that."

The top of the vanity is covered in the same 1" (2.5 cm) glass mosaic tiles that are on the walls, only in a yellower green to connect the surface with the golden yellow of the lacquerware sinks. The visual play of the three colors reinforces the oceanic feel of the space while also turning the sinks into a focal point. The birch plywood cabinet doors were stained deep walnut to contrast with the lively greens of the tiles. The brushed-nickel knobs are just big enough to grab onto without interrupting the smooth plane of wood.

"I love that bathroom," says Mitchell, of the completed project. "Because the house is so narrow, you don't expect to see this kind of bathroom in the house. And because it's located on the top floor, it's always filled with sun."

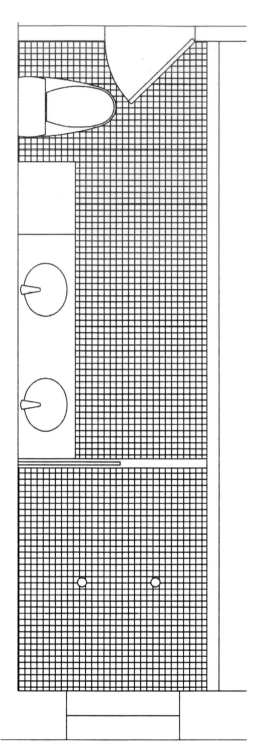

ABOVE: Floor plan

OPPOSITE TOP: Inexpensive lacquerware bowls from Asia turn the vanity into something special. Many bowls can be repurposed in this manner, though ones that easily chip are probably not ideal for high-traffic bathrooms.

OPPOSITE BOTTOM: A tiled recess in the wall provides a convenient place to store bath products without distracting from the clean lines of the design.

SINKS AND FAUCETS:

To make a pair of inexpensive sinks, Mitchell repurposed $28 lacquerware bowls by drilling holes in them and outfitting them with drains from George Taylor Specialties. For surface protection, he added a few coats of lacquer. In place of expensive fittings, he found a pair of American Standard kitchen faucets at the Home Depot Design Expo that had enough reach for the high bowls, then mounted them on a diagonal.

TILES:

The floor-to-ceiling glass mosaic tiles by Bisazza are a sea-glass green called Laguna Blend. The Bisazza tiles covering the vanity top are a slightly yellower green, which acts as a visual bridge between the green of the wall and the golden yellow of the sink bowl.

HIS AND HERS

by Studio Ethos

LIGHTING:

A wooden sconce by Santa & Cole, chosen to match the teak vanity, provides a soft, diffused light for applying makeup in the mirror beside it (not shown). Recessed lighting was strategically placed to avoid shining directly from above, which can make a person look tired. Dimmer switches control the flow of light, softening the mood or increasing illumination as needed.

SHOWER:

The shower doors are made of tempered Starphire glass, which is crystal clear. It was sandblasted for a frosted finish, giving it the appearance of ice. The shower is covered with slabs of the same honed Jerusalem limestone used on the floors and countertops. Natural light streams in from a skylight above, while a teak bath mat from Waterworks adds warmth on the floor and minimizes slipping.

FITTINGS:

Angular polished-chrome Hansgrohe fittings (from the Axor line) were used for the shower, sink, and tub, unifying the three areas of the bath that have to do with cleansing. The tub in the corner is the Bath Edition 2 by Philippe Starck.

To create a bathroom that's contemporary but not cold, Studio Ethos juxtaposed such sleek, modern fixtures as the Philippe Starck tub with warm teak cabinetry and an antique, red Chinese chair (not shown). Colliding old and new objects can soften the look of a space, making it more sensual.

If you're the type of person who agonizes over what design style to embrace or can't commit to a certain look, take a cue from Studio Ethos, the Los Angeles-based design firm that created this tranquil retreat for a Beverly Hills couple to share. "We don't really focus on achieving a particular style," says cofounder Abboud Malak. "We're more interested in how something feels than how it looks, and from this point the style evolves." To which his business partner Kelly Schandel adds: "It is important to us that the spaces we design have soul—in other words, they evoke a certain emotion upon entering them."

The bathroom suite is a long, narrow space that is really two adjoining bathrooms (his and hers) connected by a shared shower. Each room has its own entrance and is fitted with a custom teak vanity, mirrors, glass shelving, and a WC; hers also has a bathtub, which has been angled into the corner so that the bather is enveloped by the room while bathing. "Our goal was to create a soothing environment," says Malak. "We wanted it to be a sanctuary."

To establish a feeling of serenity and create a timeless look, the designers chose calming, neutral materials such as honed Jerusalem Gold limestone for the countertops and floors and Venetian plaster on the walls. For the vanities, they went with a quarter-sawn teak, which has an interesting grain pattern and an organic presence. The wood is protected with a clear coat of polyurethane. "A high-gloss lacquer would have diminished the organic feel of the natural wood," says Schandel. "We wanted the finishes to be as muted and subdued as possible to maintain the space's serenity."

Carefully planned lighting is an integral part of the design. "One of the most important things in the bathroom is lighting," explains Malak. "People tend to think of it last and end up with poor lighting. You need to consider from the beginning how you will use the space and choose the lighting type accordingly." The designers always plan where to put a bathroom's lighting as soon as the floor plan is finished; then they source and specify the fixtures they want even before construction begins. This ensures that light fixture locations are taken into consideration during construction.

"Once we address the practical considerations, then we focus on designing something that is both inspiring and timeless," says Schandel, summing up their approach. "Something that will still move you in 20 years."

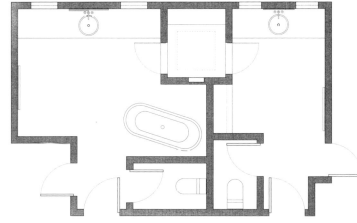

Floor plan

A STEELY CALM

by ColePrévost

When renovating the D.C.–area home of a Washington lobbyist, husband-and-wife design team Robert Cole and Sophie Prévost allowed the minimalist sensibilities of their client to dictate the top-floor overhaul. What were formerly two bedrooms, one bath, and one closet became one open 420-sq-ft (39 sq m) loft area centered on a simple palette of black and white in shiny textures. Taking down all but the exterior walls and removing the insulation in the attic transformed the space into more of a "great room" than an upstairs bedroom.

The client, originally from Montana, wanted a sense of openness in the master suite that is difficult to come by inside the Beltway. ColePrévost created a floor plan inspired by Montana's vast, open plains but with a distinctly urban interior style. Choosing colors and materials that take their cue from metropolitan skylines rather than pastoral landscapes, the designers used slick surfaces throughout the bathroom and kept the color palette to a blend of blacks, whites, and grays. Polished-chrome and sleek porcelain fixtures add an industrial quality to the space, while geometric accessories and a flat-screen television, suspended from the ceiling, add a futuristic flair.

Separated from the bedroom by a translucent wall of acid-etched glass, the space retains a sense of openness while meeting the need for privacy. In order to demarcate the bathroom, the floor in that area was raised by 4" (10.2 cm). Seen from the sleeping area, the highly stylized soaking tub is perfectly framed by the sandblasted glass and elevated to a level of sculptural artwork.

ColePrévost designed a carefully arranged lighting plan that is not only functional but allows for dramatic lighting effects in the evening. The translucent-glass wall is cleverly lit with wall washers that can make the glass more reflective (and less transparent) or it can work like a theatrical scrim to emphasize the silhouettes of figures in the bathroom. Indirect spotlights installed in the open ceiling beams are used as task lighting over the sink and add to the contrast of light and darkness already in play with the black-and-white color scheme. "The client wanted a 'knock 'em dead,' cool-looking place," says Cole. "We did our best to meet that and also keep it practical and functional."

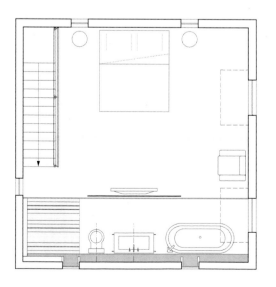

LEFT: Floor plan

OPPOSITE: The view into the bathroom from the sleeping area shows the acid-etched glass wall that creates privacy while keeping the lofty master suite open and free from clutter. The bathtub becomes more like a work of art when elevated on a glossy black floor and lit dramatically with indirect spotlights and candlelight. A flat-panel television is hung from the rafters to be viewed from the sleeping area.

INDUSTRIAL FLOORING:

The floor was originally designed with highly textured, dark brown tiles, but the client wanted it to be sleek and shiny black instead. ColcPrévost revisited the design, substituting an industrial flooring product similar to thick rubber tiles. Finished with a clear urethane coating, the overall effect is a slick, uniform surface.

ACID-ETCHED GLASS:

For an evenly translucent effect, this type of glass is a top choice when designers are looking for semiprivate room dividers. Obscuring the details but hinting at what's behind, acid-etched glass can separate rooms without sacrificing light. Here, the designers added recessed lighting to wash the glass wall like a theatrical scrim, making it appear more opaque to those watching television on the other side.

To create a sense of openness in this master suite, the designers eliminated all of the walls. As a result, the bathroom was relegated to a long, narrow strip along the western exterior wall. This meant that all of the fixtures—bathtub, sink, toilet, and shower—had to be lined up along one wall for plumbing purposes. ColePrévost solved this dilemma by choosing sleek, streamlined fixtures with strong vertical lines arranged, one right after the other, along the length of that wall. In alternating materials— black-painted wood, white enamel, polished chrome—the highly sculptural pieces add visual interest, and the overall effect feels like a row of sculpture, strengthened by the repetition.

"Everything had to be tight," explains Cole, "and the client wanted it to be as clutter-free and open as possible, so keeping it quiet-looking was the challenge." Choosing minimalist fixtures from Dornbracht and fittings from Axor helped keep the shapes from becoming too distracting. The repetition of coordinating styles and forms also subdues the hard-working bathroom wall, making it feel more orderly. The simple lines of the oversized soaking tub and the vertical design of the toilet play off of each other, directing the eye toward the shower area.

Beginning with the long, low soaking tub, the fixtures become gradually taller with each step toward the shower—and each one complements the next. The polished-chrome freestanding sink plays off the curvaceous heft of the tub with its open and rectangular framework; a curve in the basin, however, refers to both the tub and the next fixture in line, the toilet. Combining a tall, angular tank with a round bowl, the toilet makes a perfect match for the sink and free-standing storage unit. A tall, skinny showerhead stands at the far end, calling attention to the matching Starck-designed chrome accents on each fixture: the toilet flusher, sink mixers, and tub filler.

"There's a sense of repose, sobriety, and quiet," says Cole. "It needed to be a place for the clients to relax and chill." This clean-lined bath remains serene and monochromatic by keeping storage close at hand but concealed in a freestanding black cabinet, which also eliminates the need for a medicine cabinet. Instead, the mirror over the sink conceals incandescent lighting tubes that illuminate the sink area while washing the wall around the mirror with a warm glow. Flowers, candles, and other sculptural accents can be displayed on the granite windowsill that extends to the sink. The rest of the surfaces are kept free and clear of all bathroom supplies.

MIRROR:

The designers created a mirror with integral lighting in an effort to streamline the vanity area. On
the back of an oversized mirror, 6" (15.2 cm) of
the silvering were stripped away on three sides.
Incandescent tube lighting was installed behind the
mirror to illuminate the sink area.

SINK:

In highly polished chrome, the modern curved
sink from the OXO Collection sits in a chrome
freestanding washstand. One of the more difficult
materials to keep clean, chrome must be wiped
down after each use to eliminate water spots. The
faucet and mixers, from Axor, coordinate with
the adjacent toilet flusher.

ABOVE: A polished-chrome basin sits on a freestanding frame
of the same material. Bath accessories are kept hidden
(with the exception of a slablike soap dish) in the nearby black
storage cabinet.

The far end of the bath is designated as the open shower area. Created to resemble an outdoor shower, the entire space was designed to accommodate splashing and to dry quickly. Cole planned a 4 x 5' (1.2 x 1.5 m) area with a hollowed-out floor basin lined with tiles. Duck boards, or slatted wood rafts, were then laid down over the tile basin. A signature of Robert Cole's, these wooden shower floors are not only warm in the winter and cool in the summer but easy to clean. "We always install a handheld shower," explains Cole, "so you can just pick up the planks and hose everything down."

The walls around the shower were cleverly fabricated from a material used for freeway signage. Before pigment is added to it, glass-reinforced plastic (or GRP) looks amazingly like rice paper. It is also highly durable and semitranslucent. ColePrévost used the material to create a sculptural box around three sides of the shower. This not only creates a waterproof barrier from the

bedroom but also a light box effect when lit with the specially designed floor lighting: Leaving a 1' (30.5 cm)-wide space between the GRP and the outside walls, Cole placed wall washers in the floor to illuminate the material and indirectly light the shower area. Track lights hang along the ceiling beams for additional lighting.

The spaciousness of the bathroom and the openness of the plan make the issues of steam a minor problem. Still, should the room become filled with steam, the materials will be unharmed as porcelain, chrome, rubber, granite, and GRP are all water-resistant. When designing an open-plan bathroom that includes a wet area for the shower, special considerations for the durability of fabrics and materials—both in the bathroom and bedroom—must be taken. In this case, the nearly indestructible materials palette and minimalist color scheme create an industrial-strength design that is impervious to the elements.

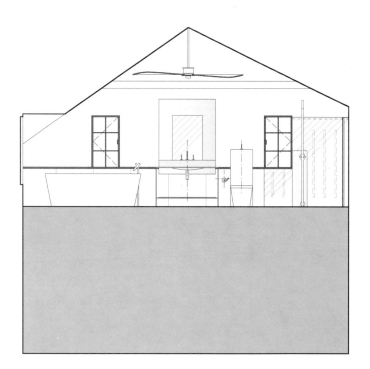

ABOVE: Interior elevation

OPPOSITE: Surrounded by walls of the material used for highway signage, this open shower area calls to mind an outdoor shower. Fitted with two "rafts" of wooden slats, the 5 x 4' (1.5 x 1.2 m) space has a showerhead reminiscent of a spigot. Without ceiling or door, the entire space can get wet without issue.

DUCK BOARD FLOORING:

Normally used for nautical purposes or decking, slatted wooden floors are treated for water resistance and placed over a shallow tiled shower basin. They provide warmth underfoot in colder months and can be hosed down and removed easily for cleaning.

GRP:

Glass-reinforced plastic is a lightweight material much like fiberglass and is primarily used for making highway signs. Without added pigments (which are used to create the signage), the material looks much like rice paper. As a lightweight, semitranslucent, waterproof material, it's perfect for shower walls and room dividers when natural light is at a premium.

LIGHTING:

When lit from behind, the GRP glows, and the walls become a kind of futuristic shoji screen separating the shower from the master bedroom. ColePrévost installed floor washers to light the outside of the shower box and create a lantern effect.

ROOM FOR TWO

by John Colamarino

LIMESTONE:

A French gray limestone is used in several places (as well as for the flooring on the entire ground floor). The bathroom floor is covered with 16" (40.6 cm) square tiles, and the tub, shower, and all of the surrounds are cut from slabs. Radiant heat provides warmth underfoot during the colder months.

TUB AND FITTINGS:

The white whirlpool tub by Kohler is oriented so that the homeowner can enjoy the view while bathing. The curved polished-chrome faucet is by Dornbracht, as is the handheld shower, which can be used to wash off sandy feet without getting wet or to rinse the tub after a bath. A grab bar facilitates getting in and out of the deep tub.

ABOVE: The long, narrow layout is completely opened up by orienting everything in the bathroom toward the view, which is maximized by a window that spans almost the full length of the room. The other exterior wall is closed off for privacy from neighbors and provides a place for hanging art. The three framed sketches are studies for sculptures by a local artist.

When architect John Colamarino first created this bathroom, located in a summer house on Cape Cod, Massachusetts, for a client, he didn't realize he'd be spending time there himself. But when he married her a few years later, that's exactly what came to pass.

The bathroom is the master bath in a contemporary house, designed and built by the architect to replace an older home that had stood there. Because the property is right on Buzzards Bay, his client wanted him to configure the interior spaces to maximize the view. "It's the most important bathroom in the house," says the architect, "and the only one with that view. We did about five or six variations, and this one wasn't even the nicest. But it was the best one in terms of the view."

The bathroom and all of the fixtures are oriented toward a window that runs almost the entire length of the room. The shower is encased in ½" (1.3 cm)-thick tempered glass, so that even in the shower, the homeowner can experience

being on the ocean. The only spot not open to the view is where the mirror hangs over the vanity. Made as tall as the window, the mirror was designed to be a continuation of the glass for a totally seamless look.

Another seamless extension is the limestone slab that tops the storage unit under the window and joins the tub decking in a long, smooth expanse of gray. Not only does it provide a surface on which to set towels and bath supplies while bathing, it can double as seating right by the window. Built-in drawers below are faced in sycamore, the honey-colored hue of the wood offering a pleasing contrast to the gray stone. The soothing, natural tones of the materials link the room to the shoreline, bringing the tranquility of the outdoor scene inside.

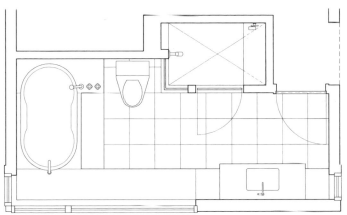

ABOVE: Floor plan

LEFT: A white rectangular Kohler sink is undermounted in the gray limestone vanity top for an integrated look, while the curving arm of the Dornbracht faucet adds height and sparkle. For light at the sink, the architect floated a pair of recessed stainless-steel lighting fixtures on either side.

SMALL SPACES

Coming to terms with a small bathroom is probably the most common experience people have when renovating, especially in older homes, where bathrooms tend to be modestly scaled. Planning how you're going to use space is even more important when it's limited. Wall-mounted sinks and toilets are a good choice because they take up less room and have a streamlined appearance. Many such sinks come with storage or a little bit of counter space for placing toiletries. As you plan, keep in mind that you'll need to maneuver around the fixtures, so be sure to calculate room for standing at the sink, sitting on the toilet, and opening the shower door. (You can check the manufacturer's recommendations for clearance or consult a contractor or designer.) If you're not a person who loves baths, consider doing away with a tub and putting in a bigger shower with a rainmaking showerhead or spray jets for an indulgent experience to start or end your day. Where space is extra tight, tucking the shower into a corner and adding an angled or curved front is a space-saving trick that also looks more dynamic than squaring off the corners. Or if you love a good soak, a freestanding tub is a visually light option, while a built-in can be tucked into a niche against a window or even in a corner.

In terms of decor, there are no hard and fast rules. Some designers recommend going with white or light-reflective colors to create the illusion of more space while others see a small bathroom as an opportunity to go a little crazy with color. Either way, a small space can offer a chance to splurge on materials, as whatever you do choose, you won't need to buy a lot of it. A backsplash of mirrored Venetian glass tiles or a small slab of statuary marble for your vanity top adds a luxurious touch, while high-end fittings or a special sink can make the space more complex and interesting. Shower curtains, bath mats, and towels can add splashes of vivid color and pattern or, in neutral tones, nubby or silky textures. The key is to make your bathroom, whatever its size, an inviting room that fits your needs.

For his client's Manhattan powder room, interior designer Wayne Nathan embraced a bold color scheme, hiring a decorative painter to reinterpret frescoes in France's Villa Kerylos (a wealthy man's replica of an ancient Greek villa). The room is filled with luxurious metal details, including custom-made designs, such as the bronze lion's-head faucet and silver sink bowl. Nathan also modified the Philippe Starck toilet with a new silver tank lid and a seat cover that's bronze outside, silver inside. Taking advantage of the tiny room's 12' (3.7 m) ceilings, he installed a dramatic Vernon Panton chandelier. "It's 3' (0.9 m) around," he says, "so when you look up, it fills the room."

FROSTED LOFT

by Chelsea Atelier Architect

For the renovation of a New York City loft, design firm Chelsea Atelier gutted the entire space and started over. Principal architect Ayhan Ozan explains how starting from scratch allowed them to create a dream bathroom for their client, a single professional woman: "We gutted the whole loft and designed the space completely around her personality and character. She's a person who works a lot and also entertains often, so the master bath was essential to her well-being. It's a place of ritual and that needed to be said in a very special way."

And a special place is exactly what the architect created. Ozan elevated a 125 sq ft (11.6 sq m) area just off of the master dressing area and enclosed the space in frosted glass, so that it feels both cozy and open. Outfitted almost entirely with designer fixtures and fittings, this tiny space was treated with as much care as any other area in the loft. Perfectly placed recessed lighting, customized furniture, and storage areas that allow for uncluttered simplicity and beautiful displays make this bathroom into something of a jewel-box within a larger space that is as stylish as its Park Avenue address.

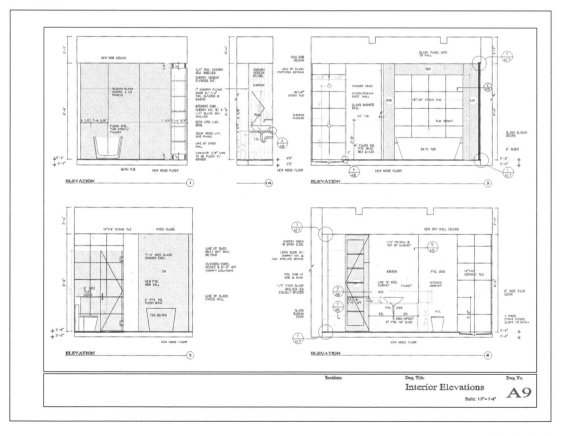

ABOVE: Interior elevations

OPPOSITE: Ayhan Ozan designed this small but spacious master bathroom for a New York City loft using designer fixtures and fittings and customizing the layout to fit the needs of a busy homeowner.

FITTINGS:

The sink faucet is by Dornbracht. The two-handled mixer used for the tub, designed by Philippe Starck, is reminiscent of a forked river. Commissioned by Hansgrohe, the simple style in classic chrome is meant to complement the sleek lines of the Duravit fixtures.

SINK AND TOILET:

From Duravit's Starck 2 collection, the basin sink and freestanding toilet are a modern and stylish option that enhances the effect of the breathtaking tub.

BATHTUB:

The clean lines and oversized dimensions of this soaking tub from Duravit make it the perfect combination of luxury and style. Designed by Philippe Starck in his second edition of bath fixtures for Duravit, the P.S. Edition 2 became a classic almost immediately after its debut.

The architect used as much glass as possible throughout the apartment to maintain an open, lofty, illuminated atmosphere. The bathroom was designed with a special type of glass that affords privacy and still lets in light. The glass is acid-etched, meaning both sides have been finely treated in an acid bath to create a subtle sand-blasted effect that is both soft to the touch and evenly light-diffusing. An added benefit of this treatment is that it resists fingerprints, which makes it the ideal material for an application where function rules. The three panels that separate this bathroom from the bedroom and dressing area were designed to allow the home-owner to close one, two, or all three panels depending on her privacy needs.

The entrance to the bathroom, just off the master bedroom's dressing area, was created using three glass panels on sliding tracks. The purpose was to give the homeowner a variety of privacy options—she can close off the bathroom entirely or just the bathtub area by simply moving the tactile acid-etched glass panels. When triple-layered, the glass has another benefit: It creates a soothing translucent color reminiscent of sea glass or clear pools of water

The highlight of this bathroom is clearly the bathtub area. Designed to feel like center stage, the Starck tub from Duravit is set against a backdrop of pale limestone. Inspiring luxuriously long soaks, the bathing area was made to feel special with a circle of tiny pinhead halogen lights overhead, directed to warm and spotlight the bathing area. Acting as both backsplash and backdrop, the wall was designed to give depth to the area and create a kind of stage for the magnificent tub. The architect did this with a freestanding structure supported with inner steel columns that was then wrapped in ¾" (2 cm) slabs of French limestone. Smaller than the actual dividing wall, the limestone structure appears to be itself framed by the glass that surrounds the top and sides.

A glass-enclosed shower at the rear of the bathroom is made of the same French limestone used behind the bathtub. To suggest the appearance of a larger space, clear glass, instead of the etched variety, was used for the shower. Another method for maximizing the limited space was the use of an open counter for the sink. Made of the same cherry as the floors, and dyed slightly darker to differentiate the two surfaces, the counter is a thin outline that practically floats on the wall. Storage would normally be located in under-cabinets built into the vanity, but in this case, it's located in hidden medicine chests on the wall adjacent to the sink. For added storage and the opportunity to display beautiful bath products, an acid-etched glass étagère was designed just inside the entrance.

LIGHTING:

Using a combination of pinhead lighting—small halogen spotlights recessed behind tiny cutouts—and other recessed halogen lighting, the designer was able to create the most versatile lighting plan. All lights are dimmable and can be controlled in sections so that the homeowner can illuminate just the tub, just the sink, or have a low-level nightlight.

FRENCH LIMESTONE:

Slabs of French limestone, a unifying factor for this bathroom, delineate the bathing areas from the rest of the space. Designed more for style than practicality, the backdrop for the bathtub and the cladding in the shower offer a kind of Roman bathlike atmosphere to this city bathroom.

OPPOSITE: Behind the tub, a free standing wall of French limestone serves as a backdrop to declare this the most special spot in the apartment. Overhead, mini-halogen lights spotlight the stage.

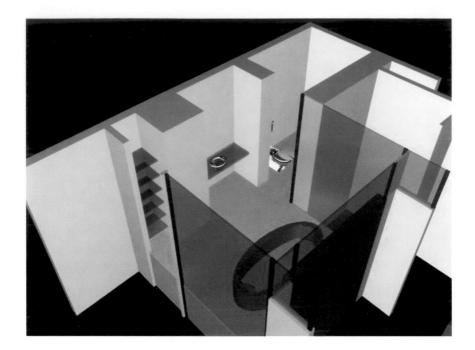

As a way to maximize light while still creating smaller areas, the architect used different types of glass throughout the loft. "Glass is an excellent material," explains Ozan. "It is easier to maintain than any of the others, including wood, marble, even painted surfaces. Glass is very practical, in my opinion. A squeegee works well to keep it clean and so does a paper towel and glass cleaner."

When choosing glass, Ozan looked at a variety of types available and chose the most practical in terms of privacy, practicality, and safety. For its transparency and durability, he used clear tempered glass—tempered meaning it has been heat strengthened in a kiln for durability—for areas like the shower and throughout the public areas of the house. He then chose acid-etched glass for areas where privacy was needed but light couldn't be sacrificed.

The homeowner needed another bathroom for guests when she entertained, so the architect designed a simple half bath located on the other side of the shower wall. (See plan above.) It is separated from the master bathroom by the same acid-etched glass that defines other private spaces in the loft.

"You can see shadows and objects through the glass so the space feels larger," explains Ozan, "but you cannot make anything out. It lets in light and diffuses it very smoothly and evenly, which makes it a nice, clean look for walls."

An aesthetically pleasing choice, acid-etched glass is also easy to maintain as the etching process creates a protective surface on the glass. "When you touch unprotected glass," says Ozan, "you'll see fingerprints and marks. This type of glass has a very fine treatment which makes it slightly porous, so you don't even see fingerprints. It's also very soft to the touch and diffuses light beautifully. We made a purposeful decision to use this type of glass; it's an excellent choice if you are looking for something nice and clean that doesn't require a lot of maintenance."

ABOVE: The entrance to the bathroom
shows the view from the master
bedroom—through the customized
dressing area. Three rectangular
panels of acid-etched glass
move on tracks to offer a variety of
privacy options.

A WORKING BATH

by MESH Architectures

It's hard to believe that the bathroom in this Brooklyn town house was once the 5 x 7' (1.5 x 2.1 m) rectangle standard in many New York apartments. Reconfigured with more square footage, a bathtub housed in an open acrylic-and-wood chamber, and oversized sliding Panelite doors, its lofty modern presence belies its humble origins.

To increase the bathroom's size, MESH Architectures took space from an adjoining bedroom and turned that now smaller room into a study. But to create the sense of spaciousness, they opened up the transitions between the rooms. "The homeowner wanted the bath to be special," says Eric Liftin, the firm's principal. "The process of reconfiguring the space led to the idea that the tub itself could be almost like a room unto itself—a chamber providing a soft barrier between the rooms."

In its new configuration, the tub occupies both rooms, so Liftin joined them by using like materials: Sandstone tiles cover the floors and the desktop in the study is made from the same synthetic slate used for the sink. "There's a symmetry there," he says. "The bath is really the inverse or twin of the study." Another link

between the rooms is provided by the computer, which sits on the desk in close proximity to the tub. While relaxing in a bath, the homeowner can access the Internet or email via a waterproof keyboard. "We started off with the concept of the bathtub in its own space like a canopy bed, open to both the study and the bathroom," says Liftin. "Then we had the idea that you could be in the tub and doing other things, like being on the computer. This creates a kind of experience that transports you. The space of the bath can be anywhere."

The tub environment is enhanced through the use of color-changing LED lights, which can be programmed using a computer to display such varied effects as patterns, strobing, or slower, more subtle shifts in color and intensity. Interactive lighting is a key part of the design and a kind of signature for Liftin, whose other projects have included moveable LED lights mounted on magnets and attached to a metal panel and fluorescent lights used behind translucent floors and ceilings. "The experience of the tub is broadened," he explains, "because the lights are adaptable for different situations when you might use the space in a different way."

OPPOSITE: Although the tub is in its own enclosure, the open sides and moveable end panels make it more of a soft barrier between the bathroom, study, and kitchen area, thus opening up the whole space rather than closing it off.

TUB ENCLOSURE:

The tub is a Thermo-masseur bath by Ultra. It
works by pumping air (instead of water) through
dozens of small jets. "It's the same principle as an
air hockey table," says architect Eric Liftin. "The
little microjets provide a better massage experience." The tub sits inside a custom enclosure,
which is clad in Hinoki cedar, an aromatic wood
that's naturally rot resistant and is traditionally
used to make Japanese soaking tubs. He found a
supplier in Oregon over the Internet.

LIGHTS:

Programmable LED lights (by Color Kinetics) are
tucked behind blue acrylic paneling called Acrylite.
Liftin created eight programs, which the homeowner can set using a simple controller. "Light
has a huge effect on your perception of a room,"
he explains. "This system is both illumination
and a display. As the colors change, your
perception of the room is changed." Plus, the
lighting can be altered to accommodate different
uses of the space.

The bathtub enclosure, which contains its own lighting and storage, is clad with Hinoki cedar, an aromatic, rot-resistant wood that's traditionally used to make Japanese soaking tubs. Liftin liked the contrast between the soft, tactile presence of the wood and the blue acrylic he used to make the tub decking, a lens for the lighting, and shelving. "The color of the acrylic is beautiful. It's really a very pale blue, and when it's a thin sheet, you can hardly see it," he says. "When it's thicker, it's easier to see but is still very delicate. It's a great contrast between the very soft blue of a synthetic material and the soft grain of the wood."

At the end of tub chamber (visible on page 117), a vertical panel of opaque white acrylic swivels to provide privacy while bathing. Magnets hold the panel in place when it is open. Inside the bathroom, a trough sink cantilevered from the wall does away with the distinction between sink and vanity and provides lots of room for water

to splash around. Two faucets and a large mirrored medicine cabinet offer ample room for a couple to use the space together. For times when a more traditional vanity top is desirable, Liftin built a Hinoki cedar shelf, which slides into place, creating a surface for toiletries.

Blue glass Bisazza mosaic tiles cover the walls of the shower, the structure of which reflects the same open philosophy of the room: A pair of narrow, tempered-glass panels provide definition for the stall and some water protection, but the shower is otherwise open to the room. Bathers simply step in and out without fussing with a curtain or heavy glass door. "Whenever the transitions between spaces are opened up," says Liftin, "it changes the way you use the space." This bathroom design shows this to be true on many levels, from its configuration and relationship to other rooms to internal transitions such as the movement from wet to dry and back.

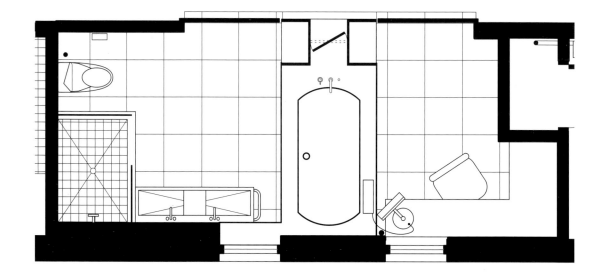

ABOVE: Floor plan showing the bathroom and study

OPPOSITE TOP: Cool and warm contrasts abound: the dark sink against the cool blue tiles, the golden cedar against the blue acrylic paneling, the black chalkboard paint (interior wall) against the Panelite doors.

SINK AND FITTINGS:

The sink is a deep trough custom made of Fireslate, a synthetic stone created for manufacturing fireplaces. Fireslate looks almost like stone but is more workable. It's available in slabs of several sizes. A removable piece of Hinoki cedar serves as a shelf for toiletries. The fittings are by Vola.

LEFT: A waterproof keyboard perches on the tub decking, allowing bathers to surf the Internet in an open, relaxed frame of mind.

PANELITE DOOR:

The oversized floor-to-ceiling sliding doors are made of Panelite, a lightweight, extremely strong, semi-transparent material with a polycarbonate core that looks something like honeycomb. It comes in panels that can be cut to size with a jigsaw, making it an easy material to work with. The panels allow natural light to filter into the room during the day; at night, when the bathroom lights are on, the doors seem to glow. "The Panelite is very beautiful," says Liftin. "And because it's translucent, it allows you to use the room itself as a lighting fixture."

LIGHTING:

The linear lights emphasize the symmetry of the bathroom and study and tie both rooms to the main space by connecting them via a shared light fixture. To make them, Liftin cut two parallel troughs into the ceiling, then laid in miniature track lights (the kind used as under-cabinet lighting in kitchens) before adding a long acrylic lens.

CHALKBOARD PAINT:

Reflected in the mirror, the interior wall is covered with black chalkboard paint—another changeable element to the design (as well as a playful reference to the homeowner's profession as a teacher). All that's needed is a piece of chalk for the wall to become a memo board or a canvas for drawings, poetry, and other forms of self-expression.

ABOVE: View of the study and bathroom from the kitchen

IN FOCUS:

SMART BATHROOMS

Technology has made its way into the bathroom in a big way, from enhancing the performance of fixtures and fittings to providing new design options and lighting environments. Flat TVs and remote controls can turn a bathroom into a movie palace, and new products such as whirlpool tubs or shower jets with programmable controls (they "remember" the water-massage preferences of various household members) make for a personal spa experience right at home.

Electronic, hands-free faucets have moved from public buildings into the home and are ideal for elderly or disabled people or children. People with arthritic hands don't have to struggle with handles, and parents never need to worry about the faucet being left running. In the shower, thermostatic valves provide temperature and water-flow control, protecting bathers from potential scalding while keeping the temperature constant and the water flowing. And multiple-jet showers now have electronic touch pads that make it easy to adjust temperature, intensity, and direction of water flow to create the perfect massage-shower experience.

Even the Internet has been brought into the bathroom, with Wi-Fi (wireless) technology allowing for free-range laptop usage and waterproof keyboards making "surfing" in the tub a viable option. "Bringing information technology into the bathroom allows you to essentially travel, using the Web to go places," enthuses architect Eric Liftin. "The bathtub is a nice medium for you to explore in because you're in a relaxed and open state. You can investigate things in a way that can lead to interesting discoveries."

Liftin also likes to use computer-programmable LED lights in his designs, which can change the ambiance with the flick of a switch and offer a wider range of options than a simple dimmer. "LED lights let you control things," he says. "They allow you to change the space in a way that keeps you from taking your environment for granted." He is a proponent of the idea that a bathroom can be more than just a place to zone out. Ideally, it can be an environment that enhances your perceptions and stimulates creative thinking. "It's easy to make a basic bathroom," he says, "everything is so standardized. It's trickier to do something in a different way that gives you a new experience every day. And you don't need a giant space to do something with technology."

Change is stimulating: Colorful new curtains or a fresh coat of paint in a bold hue can completely redefine a space. Technology can effect change—both dramatic and subtle—without requiring a lot of effort once it's been installed. "The bathroom is where ritualized activities take place, where you start and finish your day," says Liftin. "Seeing the sink opening up allows you to do things differently and that can give you a little bit of pleasure every day." And that's a feeling you can take with you to the other rooms in your life.

The floor of this half bath is made of Riverstone, clear resin tiles set with white marble pebbles. MESH Architectures gave it a technological spin by lighting it from below. "I wasn't interested in it as a regular tile," explains the firm's principal, Eric Liftin. "I liked that it was translucent, so I backlit it." First he raised the floor and built a wooden grid onto which he laid a layer of ¾" (1.9 cm)-thick acrylic sheets; then he siliconed the Riverstone tiles onto the acrylic. To light the floor, he slid small fluorescent lights into the open spaces of the grid. (They can be accessed for changing bulbs.)

FUNES HOUSE

by N Maeda Atelier

ABOVE: The angled transparent walls and ceiling of this unique bathroom reflect light coming in through the residence's many windows, activating the whole living space. As day turns to night, lights inside the bathroom change it from a reflective structure to one that casts its own glow.

OPPOSITE: In keeping with the light-catching bathroom walls and ceiling, the architect designed a glass sink and vanity, made of tempered glass for safety.

To capture something as ephemeral as sunlight, you have to stretch the boundaries of design. This is just what Japanese architect Norisada Maeda did when he created a transparent bathroom in the unconventional house known as FUNES (built for clients in Funabashi Chiba, Japan). Dramatically situated on a chunky white platform of reinforced concrete surrounded by white staircases and landings, the bathroom is all angular lines and sparkling glass surfaces. "The bathroom is one of the important spaces in a house, like the living room, entry, garden terrace, or bedrooms," says Maeda. "All the spaces in a residence should have a relationship to each other, and this is what I try to emphasize in my work."

The transparent box makes the interior space visually accessible while allowing bathers to look out at the rest of the space (the second floor of the house), which contains the living room, dining area, and a kitchen. One person can be relaxing in the tub and still chat with someone who's bustling in the kitchen or having a snack at the table. The toilet is in a separate compartment, accessed through a door that opens onto the support platform. As a nod to privacy, Maeda installed white polyester curtains (they are twisted into a roll in the photograph) but, he says, "The family doesn't use them. They don't mind being seen."

Although the bathroom is not large, it comfortably houses a deep soaking tub, an open shower, and a vanity-sink combination also built of tempered glass. Plants in white containers add splashes of verdant green and thrive in the moist environment. The walls are partially clad in white 1" (2.5 cm) mosaic tiles, while the floors are covered in larger white square ceramic tiles, which encase the entire platform and the steps leading up to the bathroom. Echoing the diagonal lines established in the larger space by the various staircases, the ceiling's strong slope also maximizes the reflection of the sunlight that cascades in through the many windows of the house.

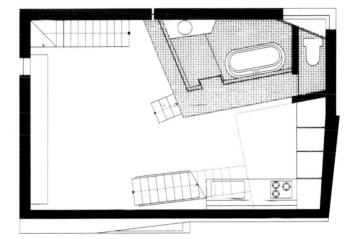

SINK AND VANITY:

To outfit the bathroom, architect Norisada Maeda used a glass sink and polished-chrome fittings from Cera Trading and set them into a vanity countertop custom made of tempered glass and supported by slim metal legs. The glass surfaces play with the light that streams through the glass walls. A simple metal lamp attached to the left of the tall, slim mirror provides task lighting at the sink. For storage, the family uses a small metal trolley.

TEMPERED GLASS:

Tempered-glass panels strengthened with safety film (a precaution against earthquakes) were used to create the walls and ceilings of the bathroom. They are bolted to a stainless-steel support frame. Glass is tempered—or toughened— by being subjected to a special heat treatment in which it is heated to about 1,250° F (680° C) and then cooled rapidly. When tempered glass breaks, it shatters into small fragments instead of jagged shards, which is why it is used wherever safety is an issue.

INDOOR-OUTDOOR BATH

by Mark Hutker & Associates Architects

"How do you get a double vanity, a dual-head shower, a bidet, a commode, and an oversized soaking tub into a bathroom that's only 10' (3 m) square?" posits Mark Hutker, the architect for this bathroom renovation on Martha's Vineyard. "Programmatically, this was the problem we were faced with. Additionally, the thing was smack in the middle of the house, so there was only one orientation—to the north."

The solution to this dilemma, conceived by the architect's firm, Mark Hutker & Associates Architects, was to create a vignette for each of the four areas of the bath: toilet, double sinks, shower, and bathtub. In so doing, they would divide the room into four discrete quadrants, making each one as private as possible without breaking up the space entirely. But for a relatively small bath, the subsequent problems of space and light became an additional concern. "You didn't want it to feel like a telephone booth when you were at each station," says Hutker. "The question became, 'How do you screen each station for an amount of privacy yet still keep it open to the overall space?'"

The firm developed a system of undulating dividers made from laminated teak walls anchored by a stainless-steel grid. Including all of the fixtures that the clients requested meant setting each one in its own corner of the square room. With these four elements already dividing the bathroom into quadrants, the placement of the partition walls was a logical next step. "In the ceiling, you can see the stainless-steel custom pieces that support the teak screen," says Hutker. "It's more sexy and more fluid to use curved lines. We couldn't move the door, but we needed something that could expand toward the window. This setup created a kind of gestural move; it embraces the view."

Taking their cues from local boatbuilders, who must consider curves and space constraints in every one of their structures, Hutker and his team chose thin strips of teak strapping to construct the dividing walls. "The whole thing is about boatbuilding," he says. "It's about being and sensing the outdoors when you're inside. It's about the art of building and using materials that last." It was also a way to create substantial partitions that would keep the room feeling light and airy. With space between the wooden slats, which are arranged horizontally, leaving room at both the top and bottom, the light reaches each quadrant and the user never feels cramped. "You sense the overall space," explains Hutker, "but you have a little bit of privacy."

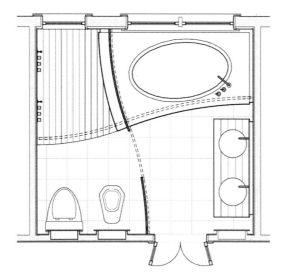 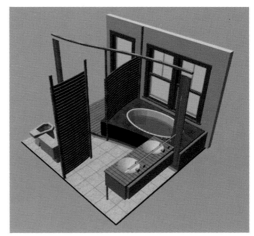

FROM LEFT: Floor plan; 3-D floor plan

OPPOSITE: "It's like the yachting sport bath," says architect Mark Hutker of this Martha's Vineyard master bathroom renovation, which combines the elements of boatbuilding with the Vineyard tradition of an outdoor shower.

TEAK:

"You don't use teak very much as an interior wood," says Hutker, "but it's just kind of fun and sporty." He chose shiplap teak—panels commonly used for boatbuilding because they overlap to create a seal when they come together—for the wall behind the bathtub. For the dividing walls, he created panels of laminated shiplap teak strapping by curving and individually screwing them to a steel frame.

VANITY:

Custom designed with teak wood interspersed with narrow strips of ebonized mahogany, the vanity sports a waterproof surface and mimics the look of the shiplap teak dividers. The architect wanted the vanity "to feel like a bench with two bowls on it." The storage unit floats on the wall and is fitted with Kohler basins and wall-mounted Kroin faucets.

SWING-ARM LIGHTING:

For task lighting, Hutker chose the stork-style design of Artemide's modern Tolomeo lamps. Mounting one over each sink, the lamps can be adjusted to offer low-voltage halogen lighting at every level.

"The goal was to build an outdoor shower experience inside," Hutker explains. He achieved this effect by first choosing materials and style elements commonly found in outdoor showers— open wooden floor grates, a copper shower basin, teak planking on the exterior wall. To maintain the nautical and natural mood throughout the space, he chose the other materials for their reference to these themes. A cleft-faced slate floor in large, uneven textures mimics the landscape outside. Tumbled-stone tiles in a watery color palette cover the apron of the bathtub. The vanity is constructed from teak with thin strips of ebony closing the gaps between the planks to suggest a look similar to the strapping on the walls.

"It's a composition of walls," says the architect, "made from materials that refer to different points on this indoor/outdoor scale." Interior walls of cool, white tile refer to the porcelain fixtures and the traditional standards of bathroom design. The exterior wall clad in teak is reminiscent of a porch or outdoor shower area, while the wood decking on the shower floor directly references this. Finally, natural slate floor tiles call out the landscaping as it continues beneath a raised platform holding both the bathtub and shower area.

With the only natural light coming from one wall with a northern exposure, the room needed lighting that could be used throughout the day but felt unobtrusive and in keeping with the informal, indoor/outdoor atmosphere. Adding low-voltage ceiling wall washers to warm the tile walls was the first step. The designers then added task lighting directly over the vanity with two adjustable lamps from Artemide that can swing out to wherever they are needed: For applying makeup, they are brought to just in front of the face; for everyday use, they remain high above the sink, providing crisp, clean light with low-voltage halogen bulbs. "The low-voltage light gives you a pure, true light color," says Hutker. "It's almost sparkling on the porcelain wall tiles, and the color temperature is more accurate than incandescent, which can be dulling."

Mirrors positioned to make the most of the light and movement hang above the vanity and over the toilet and bidet area. "The most basic problem," he says, "was that we had this phenomenal view in the window, and the only passive spot where you could actually ponder the view was the soaking tub." The firm added a mirror in the toilet quadrant to directly reflect this view and another over the vanity, adjacent to the window, to play off the view and create movement when lit with the wall washers and other lighting. "All of these mirrors," says Hutker, "really expand the sense of the space in a huge way."

PORCELAIN WALL TILE:

A cool, clean counterpart to the warm teak wood, 4¼" (10.5 cm) porcelain square tiles from American Olean cover the interior walls and discreetly refer to the bathroom's fixtures.

MOSAIC TILE:

Echoing the view of Vineyard Sound just outside the window, ¾" (1.9 cm) tumbled marble mosaic tile in shades of watery blues and greens were selected for the curvaceous tub surround.

SLATE FLOORS:

Cleft-faced American slate in 12" (30.5 cm) square tiles were laid for the flooring. The slate floor runs beneath the raised wooden decking that supports the shower area and appears to extend beyond the exterior walls out into the landscape.

OPPOSITE: As a way of bringing the bath a sense of openness and a feeling of being outdoors, the architect chose materials that created a transition between indoor and out—porcelain, wood decking, slate—and colors reminiscent of the nautical theme—oceanic blues, foamy white, warm teak wood tones, deep grays.

"The concept of showering outside is just fun," says Hutker, who originally designed this bath to connect with an outdoor shower just off the interior one. With permits and budgetary constraints limiting that design, he was determined to bring that experience inside. By creating an extra-wide shower space that expands toward the center of the room, he was able to include twin shower heads for a dual shower experience. A curtain, installed along the same metal framework that holds the teak dividing walls, can close off the shower for privacy. It can also be left open as the whole space—designed with shipbuilding materials—is highly waterproof and durable. Says Hutker: "It's the essence of the Vineyard tradition of an outdoor shower that you can enjoy all year round."

SHOWER CURTAIN:

For privacy, a standard vinyl shower curtain hangs from steel framework on the ceiling that is also the support for the dividing walls. If the interior shower is being used, the curtain is not necessary as a splash guard.

TWIN SHOWERHEADS:

Matching handheld shower fittings from Kroin are set into a porcelain wall for a double shower that is separated from the rest of the space by a curved wall of laminated teak.

WOODEN DECKING:

The floor of the shower is raised off the slate with a platform made from wooden exterior decking. Water falls through the decking and is caught by a copper basin below the platform.

ABOVE: The quadrant housing a double shower is separated from the rest of the bath with a curved wall divider at a height that allows privacy but maintains a sense of openness. The architect was able to carve out space for this luxurious shower by installing twin showerheads, side by side, on the interior wall.

IN FOCUS:

OUTDOOR SHOWERS

With a longstanding tradition of beachside living that welcomes bathing outside and rinsing off sandy suits, Martha's Vineyard is the ideal setting for an outdoor shower; Mark Hutker and Associates Architects have mastered the recipe for designing this experience. The first step is to pay careful attention to issues of privacy, lighting, and durability. If privacy is a concern, walls can fully enclose the bather; if not, and if the goal is to take advantage of a spectacular view, partial walls or no walls at all are another option. For this example, designed by Hutker, the mahogany outdoor shower was intended to be an extension of the master suite, located in an adjacent garden. "The private setting allowed for the shower to be intimately involved with the ocean view beyond," says project architect Phil Regan. Being mindful to take best advantage of daylight and offer alternatives for evening use, the walls should be constructed of durable and weather-resistant materials or hardwoods such as teak or mahogany and treated with an additional coat of weatherproofing. The showerhead, whether freestanding or mounted, can easily transform an ordinary experience into the extraordinary with large-diameter options that re-create the effect of rainfall.

LONDON COZY

by Kelly Hoppen Interiors

With its bay window and architectural moldings, this small bathroom already had a lot of charm when Kelly Hoppen redesigned it as part of a complete renovation of her London flat. She maximized that charm by placing the tub right in the window, where the curved wall seems to embrace the rounded lines of the creamy white fixture. "I love to bathe," says the designer. "I wanted the bath by the window so I could lie and look at the garden."

"I was very inspired by Japanese ceremonial style," she says, of giving the bath pride of place. She chose the tub for its old-fashioned look but modernized it by resting it on large sculptural blocks of wood. The graceful piece is surprisingly dynamic, balancing old and new, dark and light, rounded and square. "There is lighting underneath," she explains, "which gives it the appearance of being 'lifted' as though it is floating." It also adds a warm glow to the white limestone floors.

The room is a careful balance of modern and antique elements, with a strong focus on the tactile beauty of the materials. The sink, for example, was created from a found object. "It was an old Indian bowl that I had found," says Hoppen. "I drilled a hole through it and made it into a sink. I loved the idea of the old and new, vintage verses minimalism. And I love to include a star piece in a room to bring an interesting focal point to the space." The sink rests on top of a custom oak vanity, which has clean, almost austere lines in contrast to the organic, well-worn shape of the bowl. Matching the modern style of the vanity and keeping the visual focus on the basin is a wall-mounted faucet that is little more than a sleek curve of polished chrome.

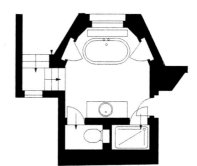

ABOVE: Floor plan

LEFT: The sink is an old wooden bowl from India that was fitted with a drain and mounted on a customized wooden vanity. The wall mounted faucet is a sleek contemporary design in a polished-chrome finish.

OPPOSITE: The many carefully chosen details in this cozy bathroom add up to an inviting space.

ROMAN SHADE:

The stylish window treatment, an off-white linen shade with a stripe of black vintage velvet, is reminiscent of the simple elegance of Japanese calligraphy and can be lowered for privacy. It was designed by Hoppen for use in the space.

TUB AND FITTINGS:

The old-fashioned tub is actually new (from C.P. Hart) and comes with no feet. Designer Kelly Hoppen gave it a sculptural presence by resting it on two thick blocks of wood. The dark, rectangular blocks offer a pleasing contrast to the pale, curved lines of the tub, while underlighting adds a bit of magic.

LIMESTONE OASIS

by Jon Andersen Design Service

Though it's nestled on the top floor of a late-19th-century town house in Boston's South End, the master bathroom designer Jon Andersen created for a client is reminiscent of a Roman bath. The room has an indulgent, spa-like quality, established through a well-planned layout and the use of rich materials such as satin nickel fittings, alabaster sconces, and the beautiful sand-colored limestone that covers almost every surface.

The first step in creating the design was the reconfiguration of the entire top floor, turning two small bedrooms and their shared bathroom into a master bedroom-and-bath suite. The bathroom became one of the key ways to get better circulation into the whole floor, which now houses a master bedroom, bathroom, office, and laundry room. Relocating it to the center of the floor and turning it into a pass-through connecting the bedroom and office not only garnered more space for the room but also placed it squarely at the heart of the suite, elevating its importance as a design element in the larger scheme of the house. "Since it is in the core of the client's master suite," says Andersen, "we wanted that feeling of richness to work with the other rooms, which are furnished with antiques and natural wool carpeting."

The only complicating factor was a lack of natural light. "Because there was no real direct light in the new location," he adds, "we knew we wanted to use light materials and provide access to indirect natural light." To maximize shared light from the surrounding rooms, he installed pocket doors, which slide completely out of sight and can be left open whenever privacy isn't an issue. And to increase the amount of natural light during the day, he added small skylights over the bathtub and shower. As for the limestone, that choice was client-driven. "He really fell in love with the sandy beige of this stone," says the designer. "It's neutral and calming and rich, all at the same time."

Although the limestone covers almost every surface—it was used on the walls to a height of 7' (2.1 m), the vanity top, doorway casings, the tub surround, shelving, and the floor—it appears in various sizes, which adds rhythmic complexity to the design. The walls are covered in 6 x 12" (15.2 x 30.5 cm) rectangular tiles and are edged along the top with a row of 2" (5.1 cm) square tiles. A single smooth slab tops the vanity, a custom piece designed by Anderson to look like a found object. And on the floor, the 12" (30.5 cm) square tiles have been placed diagonally. The effect is of a harmonious, unified whole that is nonetheless visually interesting.

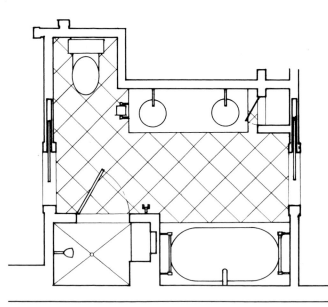

LEFT: Floor plan

OPPOSITE: Covering the walls with limestone tiles gives them more weight and presence than a painted wall would have and creates a sense that the room is a haven, a place for resting and replenishing one's spirits, as well as bathing.

LIGHTING:

The designer floated the sconces in the mirror, allowing him to maximize mirror size while still providing necessary task lighting for the vanity. The retro-style sconces are brushed nickel with creamy alabaster shades in a design called Pier by Urban Archeology.

DURANGO LIMESTONE:

Almost all of the bathroom surfaces are covered in a sand-colored tumbled Durango limestone. Old-fashioned sconces and towel hooks from Urban Archcology, along with salvaged pieces such as the antique glass knobs on the vanity and shower door, add visual richness and a sense of history.

HIDDEN MEDICINE CABINET:

The medicine cabinet is hidden behind the mirror and framed by three rows of 2" (5.1 cm) square limestone tiles. Leftover space was used to create a 12" (30,5 cm)-deep cabinet, providing plenty of storage to help keep the vanity uncluttered. A small antique glass knob installed on the mirror (added after the picture was taken) opens the door.

"One thing about 1880s bathrooms," says Andersen, "is that they were very utilitarian. We wanted to make this feel like part of the house but with more richness than it would have had, more luxurious than it would have been." And although the room is completely new, he added historical nuances such as the antique glass knobs that are used as handles on the tempered-glass shower door, on the vanity drawers, and on the mirrored door of the medicine cabinet.

And where antiques weren't available, they were created. The vanity was designed to look like a found object, with turned wooden legs and a limestone top (recalling marble-top Victorian furnishings). When it was completed, an artist was brought in to apply a faux finish, adding a patina of age to the painted surfaces. The white

porcelain sinks perch on the countertop like a contemporary spin on 19th-century washstands, while faucet and handles are a playfully retro design featuring cross handles with porcelain insets. Even the sconces add an aura of days past, with upward-curving metal arms and rounded alabaster shades evocative of gas streetlamps.

Revamping the space allowed for the separation of the bathing and shower areas, an increasingly popular choice for bathroom design. Without a shower-in-tub arrangement, a shower curtain or glass enclosure is not needed, and the bathtub niche can be left open to the rest of the room. That way, the homeowner doesn't have to climb behind a physical barrier to take a long, lazy soak in the tub and can instead enjoy the ambiance of his surroundings.

SINKS AND FITTINGS:

Though the Kohler sinks are a contemporary design, their white porcelain is reminiscent of the porcelain washstand bowls that were once a fixture in Victorian homes. Wall-mounted platinum matte faucets by Dornbracht feature retro-style handles with porcelain inlays; the name of the design is Madison. The brushed-nickel towel bar and toilet paper holder (attached to the side of the vanity; the toilet is recessed into a niche), as well as other towel bars and hooks in the bathroom are all from Urban Archeology.

VANITY:

The vanity was designed by Jon Andersen to look like a found object but still provide plenty of storage. "I wouldn't recommend trying to make a found object into something," he says. "You'll have to accept the limitations of its design (like no drawers), you'll spend ages finding it, and it might cost almost as much to have it converted." Instead, he suggests finding inspiration in an old piece but designing something new that fits the space and your needs. Antique pulls were found at Restoration Resources.

OPPOSITE: Custom-building the vanity allowed the designer to have the look of an antique and the conveniences of double sinks and plenty of storage.

ABOVE RIGHT: Three sizes of Durango limestone tile are arranged to create a patterned motif along the wall in the bathtub niche. The smooth sheen of the platinum matte Dornbracht faucet provides a sophisticated contrast to the chalky beige stone.

BELOW RIGHT: Interior elevation

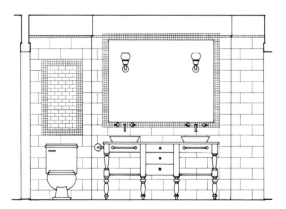

SHAKER MINIMALISM

by Austin Patterson Disston Architects

"We wanted something clean and minimal but also warm," says Stuart Disston, a principal with Austin Patterson Disston Architects and the designer of this small bathroom, located in a weekend cottage in Westport, Connecticut. "So that affected our choice of materials." The creamy white walls are painted poplar planks, the floorboards are made of fir, and the room's centerpiece is a snowy white bathtub encased in green slate. The same slate was paired with salvaged chestnut to create a vanity; the clean lines and rich materials lend the piece a timeless Shaker sensibility.

"You could almost call this bathroom style Shaker Minimalism," he says, referring to the easy blend between the modern elements and the home's cottage style. "Minimalism can be a bridge between traditional and modern styles. Both Shaker and modernism have clean lines, so those two styles can join together gracefully." A neutral palette keeps the look contemporary, while the craftsmanship of the furnishings and small details such as Pottery Barn wall sconces add nostalgic charm.

Because Disston was expanding and renovating the 1910 cottage, he was able to configure a new space for the bathroom, but he still had to work with limited square footage. And his clients' wish list was a long one: a deep soaking tub, a separate shower, double sinks, and two medicine cabinets. To fit everything, he placed the tub under the window and created adjacent cubbies for the toilet and shower off to one side.

To keep the room from feeling claustrophobic, the architect built the cubbies of glass. The WC stall is accessed through a frosted door, which has a clear transom above it. The shower stall is the same design in reverse: a clear door with a frosted transom. They are separated by a glass divider (frosted below, clear transom above), which continues the design motif and also allows the WC to borrow light from the windowed shower. "The shower and toilet area is a sort of [Piet] Mondrian grid in glass," explains Disston. "It's a neat feeling because you are in these glass cubes with a stratum around them. There's an interesting sense of architecture, and the space offers privacy while still being light and open."

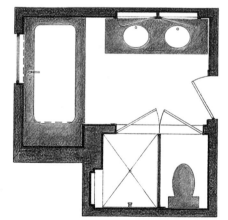

ABOVE: Floor plan

RIGHT: The toilet chamber is accessed through the frosted-glass door on the left, the shower through the clear one on the right.

OPPOSITE: Although the bathroom is a newly renovated, classic designs for the vanity and tub surround combined with cottage-y details like the sconces and a woven basket instead of a plastic trashcan make it fit right into the cottage style.

SLATE TUB SURROUND:

Undermounting the Waterworks tub (with fittings by Chicago Faucets) integrates it seamlessly into the slate surround. "Slate is a softer material than most," says architect Stuart Disston. "It scratches and shows wear. Over time it takes on its own patina, and you have to accept that. I wouldn't recommend it for anyone who expects something to look the same in 10 or 12 years."

VANITY AND SINKS:

The vanity was custom made of salvaged antique chestnut and slate from Vermont Structural Slate. The faucets on the undermounted American Standard sinks are from Chicago Faucets but were given a custom brushed-nickel finish. The built-in medicine cabinets were customized to fit the size and style of the room.

COASTAL RETREAT

by Van Dam and Renner Architects

While designing the master bathroom in a seasonal residence he built for clients on the coast of Maine, architect Sam Van Dam found himself balancing the convenience promised by modern fixtures and fittings with the rustic charm of a lodge the homeowners envisioned. "They wanted a Maine lodge, but they wanted it to be quite sophisticated technically," he says. "They wanted it beautifully finished and perfectly square. The idea was that the bathroom would have all of the clean details that would allow it to be maintained well. We needed to balance the lodge aspect of the design with the desire for modern convenience."

Douglas fir paneling on the walls and ceilings set a woodsy tone. Fir is a good choice for a bathroom because it resists moisture and has a vertical grain, which allows for consistently tight joints. "The vertical grain doesn't move around a lot," explains Van Dam. "This is especially important in Maine, which experiences extremes of temperature. With another wood, like maple, there would be a lot of seasonal movement—

particularly shrinkage in the winter." The shower is a spacious, white-tiled chamber with a modern tempered-glass door. The shower fits snugly in a corner, its exterior walls clad in Douglas fir for seamless integration into the room. And, for a sybaritic touch, the bathroom floors have radiant floor heating, so they are constantly warm underfoot.

The single light switch on the wall, with its oil-rubbed bronze cover, has an antique, hand-crafted look but is actually part of a complex, modern lighting system. "The homeowners wanted all of the lighting to be controlled with an old-fashioned switch but also have sophisticated dimming and light-grouping capacity," says the architect. "This can be difficult when you have several lights ganged together with a high total voltage. We worked with our lighting designer to put all of the modern controls in the basement." When you turn on the light, a low-voltage signal is sent to the controls in the basement where the dimmers and relays are located.

OPPOSITE: The master bathroom of this seasonal home in Maine brings to mind the famous maxim credited to Mies van der Rohe: "God is in the details." Hand-hammered door-knobs, antique lighting fixtures, and a recessed pocket for the window shade are just some of the carefully considered aspects of this casually elegant design.

VANITY AND SINKS:

The cabinetry is faced with Douglas fir and topped with a slab of mahogany, a handsome reddish-brown wood that resists water penetration. For an integrated look, the white porcelain Waterworks sink was undermounted. It is fitted with a polished-chrome Dornbracht faucet.

HARDWARE:

The door and window hardware throughout the house is from Nanz in New York, a company that specializes in high-end residential hardware. The pieces were cast of bronze, then hand-hammered and given an oil-rubbed finish. In the bathroom, the bronze light switch plates and cabinet knobs are by Sun Valley but were finished at the same plating facility as the Nanz hardware to ensure the finish would match.

TUB NICHE:

A white Waterworks tub is tucked into a windowed niche, allowing the homeowners to watch for wildlife while bathing. An old-fashioned chrome Dornbracht faucet with porcelain insets and a handheld shower add period charm. The tub decking is a slab of mahogany, while the sides are tiled in the same white squares that cover the floor and shower and are used as wainscoting on the walls. The windows throughout the house are framed in mahogany and were made by a Vermont company called Woodstone. For privacy, a roller shade located in a recessed pocket in the ceiling performs its function without interrupting the flow of the design.

ABOVE: In the adjacent dressing room, the walls are finished with smooth-to-the-touch Douglas fir while the floor is a re-sawn southern yellow pine with a slightly rough finish. "The house is brand new," says Sam Van Dam, "but it's meant to feel like a Maine lodge, so everything was chosen to tilt in that direction." Built-in cabinets to the left and right of the dormer window were carefully positioned so that the homeowners can stand while accessing them. The dormer is set high enough so that there's plenty of privacy.

"I've always liked story-and-a-half buildings," says Van Dam. "It allows the building to be lower to the ground, which is important in a natural setting. Inside, there's a sense of intimacy with the lower-sloped ceilings that people like, and there's also a lot of visual interest. You really see the geometry of the structure as the light plays on it. The only difficulty with working with these lower roofs is that you have to be very clever about how you use the space that is not full height and make sure that it's really useful and accessible." The sloped part of the ceiling was a natural place to put the tub, as people bathe while sitting; however, the architect still made sure it was possible to stand up, so that getting in and out of the tub would be easy. Placing a window in that wall opens it and brings in light. The sink and vanity face a full-height wall, which leaves room for a generously sized mirror and task lighting.

Vanity cabinets, made of Douglas fir with oil-rubbed bronze drawer pulls, are topped with a rich mahogany slab, as is the tub surround. The contractor hired a cabinetmaker who specializes in working on boats. "Someone who works on boats really understands what's required to join and finish wood so that it resists water penetration," explains the architect. "This is especially critical with an undermounted lavatory, because unless it's designed and fabricated without a great deal of care using the best possible materials, sooner or later the wood will degrade." While its natural water-resistance makes it an excellent choice for bathrooms, mahogany does require special care and should be wiped dry rather than left to dry on its own.

For help with the interiors, the homeowners hired New York designer Mariette Himes Gomez, who chose the white tiles and the antique lighting fixtures and also integrated furnishings from another house, such as the pinecone-framed mirror in the dressing room. "A really good designer understands how to make a whole out of many pieces," says Van Dam, "and this can make for a much better project." He recommends bringing an interior designer into the process early, so that he or she can work collaboratively with the architect. Of equal importance is the selection of the contractor. "In a project like this one, in which the owners were insistent on using the best and most appropriate materials and achieving the highest standards of construction, the contractor's knowledge and skill are absolutely critical to the process," he says. "Cold Mountain Builders was the right contractor for the job."

With its clean lines and generous proportions, the bathroom feels quite contemporary, even with all of its period details. "The design motif is actually fairly subtle," says the architect, reflecting on his work. "There's the lodge quality of the wood and materials, but it doesn't have a lot of ornate or complicated detail related to natural features, like unpeeled logs. It's a distilled approach, somewhat like traditional Japanese or Shaker design."

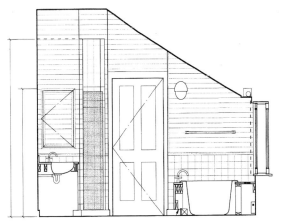

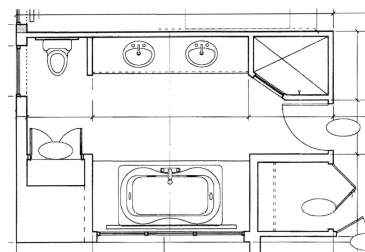

FROM LEFT: Interior elevation of master bath facing west; floor plan

GLASS WORKS

by Living Interior Design

Creating enough room for storage in a small space can be challenging, and this bathroom, renovated by Living Interior Design for a client's contemporary home, was no exception. "Originally the bathroom consisted of a tub, a toilet, and a pedestal sink," explains interior designer Celia Domenech, the company's founder. "They really needed more storage." She replaced the pedestal sink with a custom-made maple vanity that contains three drawers and a pullout laundry hamper. A pivoting mirror hides shelving for small items, and toiletries can be kept in a shower niche created for that purpose. To make room for towels and decorative items, Domenech added a niche next to the shower. The recessed rectangle gives dimensionality to the small room, an effect she heightened by adding lighting. When the light is on, the three glass shelves are illuminated, and the niche seems to glow.

With its glass-bowl sink, glass-top vanity, shower stall, and glass paneling, the bathroom has an aquatic sensibility, which provides a playful reference to the home's Miami Beach location and also filled the homeowner's request for something upbeat. Aqua 1" (2.5 cm) mosaic tiles cover the floors; they were chosen because the grout between the small tiles allows for gripping, creating a safe, nonslippery surface. The color matches the aqua blue walls of the master bedroom. "The homeowners wanted their bedroom to be refreshing and energetic," says the designer. "Continuing the same color throughout the two spaces helps join them and also makes the bathroom seem larger."

The warm, golden tones of the stained maple cabinetry add a pleasing counterpoint to the cooler tones of the glass and are picked up by the wooden Venetian blinds and teak shower bench. The bench allows the bather to be seated, which is helpful for someone who is elderly or disabled and can also facilitate other bath activities, such as drying off or shaving your legs. The bench is attached to the wall by a chrome hinge, so it can be folded up against the wall when not in use.

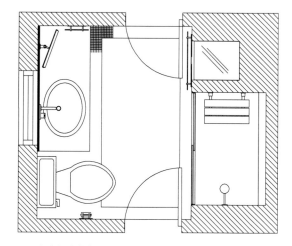

LEFT: A niche built into the tiled shower wall provides storage for bath products. The teak Waterworks bench weathers well in a wet environment.

ABOVE: Floor plan

OPPOSITE: Fresh blue tiles and blue-green glass panels bring an invigorating energy to this small master bathroom, making it a refreshing place to bathe and get ready for the day.

GLASS WALL PANEL:

The panel is made of ¾" (1.9 cm) tempered glass that has been painted white on the back. The thickness of the glass gives it its intense aqua tone. Originally, the designer had planned to fasten the glass to the wall with four 1" (2.5 cm) chrome-plated screws. But the number of openings that were already needed—the large window, as well as holes for attaching the Waterworks pivot mirror and the wall-mounted Vola faucet—was a complicating factor. To avoid the risk of breaking the weakened glass by drilling additional holes, she opted instead to use a U-channel bracket to hold it against the wall. She reduced the strain on the wall by resting the panel on the top of the vanity.

PIVOT MIRROR:

The window's location directly over the sink left no room for a mirror, so a pivoting one by Waterworks was installed in the corner. Because it was being attached to the wall through the glass panel, it was given additional support in the form of shock-absorbing foam, placed between the screws used to fasten the mirror in place and the glass panel.

UNUSUAL SPACES

Some bathroom spaces defy all categories—whether installed on the roof of a town house or hidden in a windowless basement, they offer unique challenges not generally encountered in the course of a regular renovation or design. This last chapter is filled with such rooms and the creative solutions provided by the talented designers and architects who designed them. In each case, the designer made the most of the limitations of the space—creating a moving shoji wall to open up or close off a bathroom in a corner of a bedroom, relying on plumbing pipes to provide the structure and decor for a small bathroom in a Japanese residence, or building a bathroom of glowing, translucent Panelite walls in the dark interior space of a New York loft. The six bathrooms included here seem to prove that the most challenging constraints end up inspiring the most innovative and memorable solutions.

For the ultimate luxury at work, Frederick Bland, a partner at the architectural firm of Beyer Blinder Belle, installed a bathtub in the Brooklyn office of choreographer Mark Morris, so he can enjoy a relaxing soak after a long day in the dance studio. "The inspiration was my listening to Mark talking about how he creates," says Bland. "He told me, 'The best stuff comes to me when I'm soaking in a bathtub.' I began to realize that, though fairly unusual, a bathtub right in his office would be perfect for him. It's sybaritic, but it's more than that. The whole idea came through a dancer's physical and creative needs." Shoji panels slide into pockets to open the bath to the space or can be pulled shut for privacy. In the tub niche, pure white subway tiles are crisply delineated against eye-popping raspberry walls, while at the opposite end of the color spectrum the office walls are a fierce, vibrant green.

LIGHT BOX

by MESH Architectures

As part of a floor-to-ceiling renovation of a New York City loft, MESH Architectures' Eric Liftin set out to create a bathroom that would be a stimulating and enjoyable place to be, while also bringing some definition to the large, open floor plan. "In a big loft, you always have this issue of central space that doesn't get light or air," he explains. "You want to animate that area, let it into the other rooms and vice versa as a way of involving it with the whole space."

Working where there had been no previous bathroom, Liftin started with a basic structural limitation that ultimately led him to find an inspired design solution. "It was a very old building in Little Italy," he says. "It used to be a slaughterhouse back in the day, so all the floors were made of sloping concrete. You can't go through concrete, so we had to raise up the bathroom floor to install the plumbing. This provided an opportunity to do something a little differently, and it seemed like a good plan to make the raised floor a feature."

Once he knew he needed to raise the floor, the architect began to think about how to make it interesting. Having worked with Panelite on other projects, he knew it would be strong enough to use as flooring. Its translucency made lighting it irresistible. "The idea was to create a steel platform to set the panels into," he says. "Then I decided to do it all around, so the ceiling and walls are all of Panelite. I installed lights under the floor and above the ceiling, so, except for the vanity light, all of the light comes from outside the bathroom."

To hold the walls and ceiling in place, the architect built frames of aluminum channels. The process required careful planning and exact measurements, especially because the translucent material made it tricky to keep the visible framing to a minimum. To light the panels, he made slender plywood dollies and attached small fluorescent lights to them. When a bulb burns out, the homeowners can just slide the lights from under the floor or off the top of the ceiling and replace it. The fluorescent bulbs create a soft, diffused glow through the honeycombed paneling. "Making the room translucent allows the bath to be a great experience," he says. "But it also affects the interior space of the loft. The bathroom becomes a large-scale lighting fixture, and when it's all lit up it looks like a glowing box."

PANELITE:

The ceilings, walls, and floors of this bathroom are made of Panelite, a lightweight, extremely strong polycarbonate with a translucent honeycomb pattern. To construct the bathroom, architect Eric Liftin created a steel platform to support the floor and built a frame of aluminum channels for the walls and ceilings. The Panelite comes in standard 4 x 8' (1.2 x 2.4 m) and 4 x 10' (1.2 x 3 m) sheets. "It's very easy to work with," he says. "You can cut it with a basic jigsaw."

UNDERFLOOR LIGHTING:

The raised floor was left open along the sides of the bathroom to allow for the installation of lighting. Small fluorescent lights—the kind used under kitchen cabinetry—were attached to skinny plywood dollies that slip between the floor supports. The dollies can be rolled out when a bulb needs to be changed.

OPPOSITE: When the lights are on, the Panelite bathroom in this New York City loft shines like a glass lantern.

The vanity for the sink floats on a translucent wall, on the other side of which is a library. Large rotating, sliding bookcases in the library allow the wall to be closed off: When one of the bookcases is folded against the wall, it takes away the translucency and provides a sense of privacy, when desired.

Panelite has the advantage of being easy to keep clean, making it a great choice for a bathroom. "You don't see fingerprints," says Liftin. "There's fiberglass facing on the material, and it has a little bit of texture, so it's not really slick and clear like glass. You don't notice little droplets of water that dry on nonporous materials." The panels were also used to make a floor-to-ceiling sliding door that closes off the shower when

it is in use, creating a translucent box within the larger translucent box that is the bathroom.

Providing a whimsical contrast to the room's high-tech materials is a salvaged cast-iron tub that rests on slender claw-foot feet. Its vivid orange exterior adds an invigorating jolt of color to the otherwise neutral room. Using such a heavy tub on a Panelite floor had its complications, however. "Instead of having a heavy tub sitting on the floor, it comes down on these four delicate points," explains Liftin. "That's a lot of weight on those points, so we ended up cutting holes in the Panelite and letting steel supports poke through." The supports are invisible, however, and the tub seems to float impossibly on the glowing, light-infused floor.

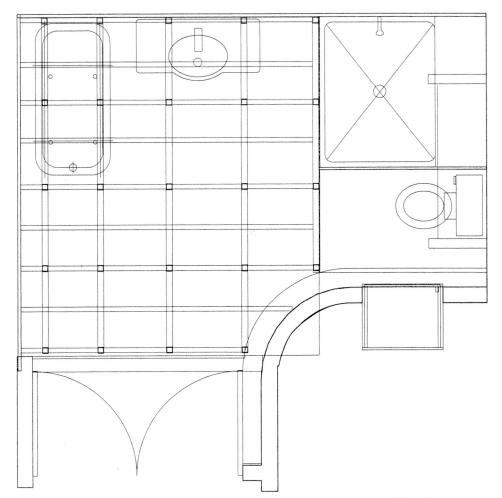

ABOVE: Floor plan

OPPOSITE: The neutral bathroom interior is enlivened by the presence of a vividly painted claw-foot bathtub.

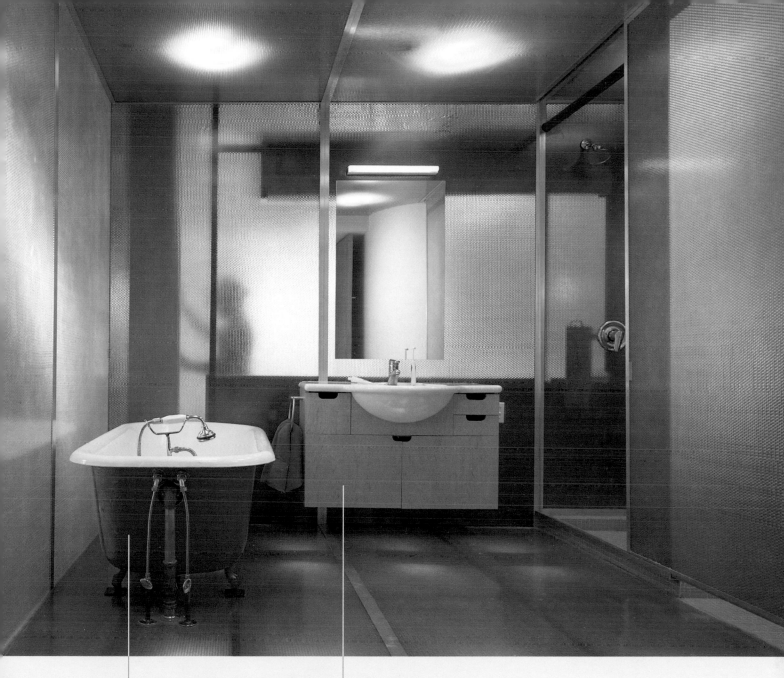

TUB:

A salvaged cast-iron claw-foot tub offers a warming contrast to the high-tech environment. For added pop, Liftin used an oil-based enamel to paint the exterior a vivid orange. To compensate for the tub's weight, he added steel supports beneath it, cutting through the floor to let the feet rest directly on them.

VANITY AND SINK:

A vanity made of a multi-ply Baltic birch plywood floats on the translucent Panelite wall. It was customized by MESH Architectures to fit the generous Duravit sink, which takes up the entire top of the vanity. The wooden cabinet is cut away in the front to reveal the curving side of the porcelain basin. The fittings are by Vola.

WATER PIPE HOUSE

by Toshihiko Suzuki

With instructions to dream up "the best and most unique design possible while meeting a small budget" for his clients' Tokyo residence, Japanese architect Toshihiko Suzuki created a doorless bathroom tucked behind a privacy screen built of repurposed steel plumbing pipes and corrugated polycarbonate sheeting. By leaving the cement floors and cinderblock walls exposed, rather than covering them with a bathroom-friendly material such as tile, he embraced the raw, industrial feel of the space. And by visibly using metal piping—an element usually hidden in bathroom construction—he gave the material a playful spin, as if the bathroom had been turned inside out.

The layout of the room is straightforward. The sink is open to the residence, while next to it, the shower and toilet have privacy behind the translucent screen. The fixtures are minimal, with the elements of their construction exposed to view. A stainless-steel sink is housed in a vanity built of metal sheeting and pipes. The shower tray sits exposed on the floor, while

a curved metal rail for the curtain (supported by a grid of pipes) is all that defines it. The curtain—a translucent white plastic that looks like a softer version of the corrugated screen—plays a double role, shielding the room from water spray and offering additional privacy for the toilet, depending how far out it is pulled. It can also be pushed against the wall between the shower and toilet to leave the room totally open.

"One of my friends uses old gas gauges and faucets for furniture," says Suzuki, when explaining his inspiration for the design. "The reincarnation of objects created by reutilizing wasted objects as materials is inspiring in different ways. Some people see the aspect of recycling in it; some find interest in the appearance of hidden and unnoticed objects of everyday life. In my case, I found hidden beauty in the pipes being a perfect system of construction." Appreciating the "purely honest and functional" nature of the metal pipes allowed him to design a unique bathroom by using an inexpensive, everyday material in innovative ways.

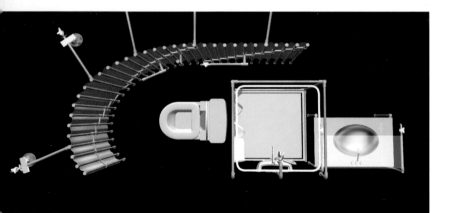

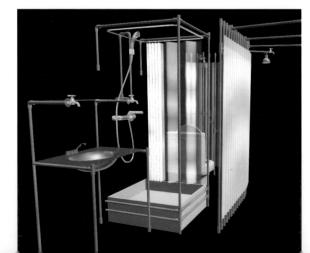

ABOVE LEFT: Floor plan

LEFT: Interior elevation showing sink and shower

ABOVE: Interior elevation showing toilet, shower, and sink

OPPOSITE: Form doesn't always follow function in this bathroom. The water pipes and spigots are repurposed as privacy screening, a shower grid, and as pure design objects.

METAL PIPES:

Metal plumbing pipes were
used everywhere: to make the
vanity, hold up the curved
shower curtain rail, and clip-on
lighting fixtures; support the
corrugated polycarbonate
screen; and as a design element.
Visible in the drawings, five
tentaclelike lengths of pipe
(ending in spigots) extend from
the screen wall into the residence. Clip-on metal lights at
the ends provide lighting in
the room and also cast light
onto the screen.

SHOWER:

In order to create a simple,
open shower, architect
Toshihiko Suzuki installed
a shower tray from INAX
directly on the cement floor,
defining the area with a grid of
metal piping and a metal
curtain rail. A translucent plastic
shower curtain adds an element
of softness to the room.

OPEN AND SHUT SPACE

by DesignARC

When architect Mark Kirkhart of the California firm DesignARC built a duplex in Santa Barbara's warehouse district, he had careful considerations for the master bathroom. Though the white stucco building with red Spanish tile was constructed as a residence, the surrounding industrial zone left the bedroom and bathroom level without much of a view. "With mostly businesses and warehouses around, there aren't any trees or gardens to look at," explains Kirkhart, "so the master bedroom and bathroom had to be more inward-looking."

In order to compensate for the lack of natural light in the master bathroom and the relatively limited space constraints, the architect designed a square room in a corner of the bedroom that could either be closed off to create a private bathroom or opened up to become part of the larger master suite. "It was a way to keep the bathroom from feeling claustrophobic," he says. "If you were bathing, you could open up the screens, and the tub would be in the middle of the space. It was also something to look at since there isn't much of a view."

With a pair of sliding shoji screens made from a welded-metal frame and translucent plastic panels, Kirkhart designed the bathroom so that two walls could slide away and create an open-plan master suite. When shut, the screens form a 90-degree angle to complete the square and close off the bathroom from the rest of the bedroom. But the screens not only serve privacy purposes, functioning as room dividers; they also function as a light source for the bathroom. "The whole purpose of the screens is that they're made of a translucent material," he says, "so that the bathroom shares the light from the bedroom."

The bathroom also borrows light from an adjacent master study on the opposite side of the wall. A high clerestory window installed at the top of that wall provides access to more natural light. Set above the mirror wall, this strip of glass seems to disappear, and it's high enough that privacy is not an issue.

Honey-toned cabinets, built by Kirkhart out of medium denisity fiberboard (MDF), offer a hint of warmth in the otherwise cool-colored bath. Finished with just a clear coat of urethane, the MDF takes on a warm hue and becomes nearly as durable as a hardwood version. The counter-tops are made from a slab of concretelike material, designed to look like slate. The result is a highly functional vanity with double sinks and plenty of storage that adds a contrasting element of warmth and natural material to the bathroom and the bedroom beyond it.

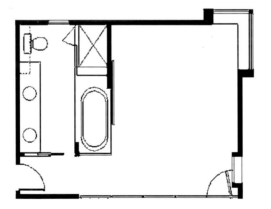

ABOVE: Floor plan

OPPOSITE: The shoji screens bring a light and airy feel to the space, offering privacy without making the windowless bathroom feel claustrophobic. A neutral palette of cool grays and white unites the two areas of the room, while the wood vanity adds a warming accent.

PAINTED GLASS:

The mirror wall behind the sink extends to the toilet area where glass that has been back-painted a soft gray replaces the mirrored surface. It not only creates added privacy but helps to camouflage and divide the toilet area.

MDF VANITY:

Architect Mark Kirkhart used lightweight and affordable MDF to create a customized storage and sink area. Fitting the clear-finished MDF cabinets with a counter of Slatescape and double stainless-steel sinks from Elkay, he was able to maximize storage and style on a limited budget.

SLIDING SCREENS:

Fabricated by Kirkhart, the translucent shoji screens were designed as pocket doors, sliding away to open the bathroom to the larger master bedroom, or sliding closed to add privacy to the bathroom. "I made them myself on-site from welded steel framing and translucent plastic panels," says Kirkhart. "I actually forced [the framing] to rust, and then I sealed it because I wanted a rustlike finish."

"The house is very small," says Kirkhart, "so I wanted to limit the color palette." Based on this logic, the architect chose a minimal scheme of natural gray, warm wood, and black slate with simple chrome and stainless-steel accents. The shoji screens complement this palette by combining black welded steel that was forced to rust before being sealed and white translucent-plastic panels. The rusted-metal finish on the metal framework contrasts with the horizontal panes of slick, white plastic; when closed, the screens serve as a graphic backdrop to the modern lines in the rest of the bathroom.

Combining a utilitarian aesthetic with a minimalist color scheme, the warm bank of storage in the vanity keeps the space from feeling cold or too industrial. To bring in stylish curves while maintaining the pared-down atmosphere, Kirkhart fitted the sink and tub with gooseneck faucets and temperature controls from a commercial supplier. "They're super-high quality and very heavy duty," he says. They are also relatively inexpensive and for the designer, who built the house for himself, limiting the budget was a key factor.

The decision to make a bathtub from a wooden frame poured with waterproof plaster was for both budgetary and practical purposes. "You couldn't pour a concrete tub on the second story of a conventional wood-framed building," he explains. "It would be too heavy, and spending the huge amount of money to make it happen would be highly impractical." Kirkhart, who knew he wanted a custom-size soaking tub big enough for two people, built a wood-frame box and lined it with plywood to create the form. He then lined it with a one-piece waterproof shell and covered it in mortar before finally pouring a ¼" (0.6 cm)-thick layer of plaster that was integrally colored to look like concrete. "Basically, the whole thing is prepared as though you were going to put tile on it," he explains. "Then you pour it with plaster, so it's essentially a small version of a wood-framed swimming pool."

"It's a great method, because if space or budget is limited, you could make this in any size or shape you wanted," he continues. "The options are nearly endless, because you aren't limited to what's on the shelf. Most standard tubs are 5' [1.5 m] long, and if you don't have enough space for that, you can do it with this style, plus it can be any depth you want, or any shape." Here, the architect chose a standard rectangular shape, but he customized the width and sloped both sides so that two people can soak comfortably. The top edge of the tub also extends beyond the bathing area into the glass-enclosed shower, where it becomes a bench or storage area. The mottled coloring of the waterproof plaster looks and feels like concrete, but he insulated the tub so it heats up quickly and stays warm long after concrete, porcelain, or plastic would cool off.

LEFT: When the screens are open, the bathtub becomes the central focal point in the room. As you enter the bedroom, the bathroom is on your left, and the tub is the only divider of the space.

OPPOSITE: With the shoji screens closed, the bathing area becomes a serene and private retreat. The plaster tub was integrally tinted to look like poured concrete, but it has a smooth, silken finish that is waterproof and insulated to keep the water warm.

COMMERCIAL FITTINGS:

Heavy-duty faucets and fittings are by Chicago Faucets, a manufacturer of commercial and industrial-quality fixtures. The high-quality, no-nonsense styling of the stainless-steel and color-coded hot and cold mixers fits right into Kirkhart's honest and affordable aesthetic.

WATERPROOF PLASTER:

For a custom-size tub, Kirkhart created a wood frame according to his dimensions and lined it with plywood and then a one-piece waterproof liner. He then added mortar and smooth-troweled it with a ¼" (0.6 cm)-thick layer of waterproof plaster called Thoroseal, which was tinted to mimic the look of poured concrete.

SLATE FLOOR TILES:

12 x 2" (30.5 x 5.1 cm) tiles of honed black slate were installed for the flooring. For the larger slab on the counter-top, the architect used a synthetic concrete product called Slatescape, which mimics the tone and texture of natural slate.

HEART OF GLASS

by Amok

To create this visually stunning shower located in a Covent Garden loft, interior designer Tanya Hudson of the London firm Amok, used a curved cast-glass wall to separate the bathroom from the rest of the living space and placed the shower right in the curve. The shimmering, textured glass is lit with angled lights in the living room as well as with lighting within the bathroom for an effect that is both dramatic and beautiful.

Hudson's design was part of a residence-wide redesign: The apartment is in a converted commercial building, and the owners wanted to revamp and update the space. The original layout had two bathrooms, but these were reconfigured to add space to the living area and create one single, large bathroom. "My clients really wanted an indulgent bathroom," says Hudson, co-founder of the London design firm Amok. "They wanted something quite rich, with mosaic tiles, and fancied the idea of a glass wall." A wall of glass blocks seemed too dated, so she suggested a pane of glass. "They actually considered having it transparent at one point," she says, "and everyone else was asking, 'Are you sure?'" Ultimately, they decided on textured translucent glass, which offered a little more privacy. Its striped texturing is a result of how it's made, a process called casting whereby the liquid laminated glass is poured into a shape that has been formed in sand. "It was actually quite complicated," says Hudson. "There were lots of issues with the glass being curved and tempered."

Inside the bathroom, the walls are covered in other forms of glass. A random pattern of 1" (2.5 cm) green glass mosaic tiles encases the chunky partial wall that separates the shower and tub. The same tiles line built-in niches created for storing bath products; they also run the length of the wall behind the tub. Against the far end of the room, tempered glass panels were attached to one wall and used as backing for the built-in wenge wood shelving. White paint sprayed on the back of the panels enhances their green sheen; it also hides the strong adhesive that holds them in place, so the effect is of floating green planes, without any metal screws to mar the illusion. "You can just stick the glass onto the wall," says the designer. "Although if your ceiling's out of square, you'll run into problems."

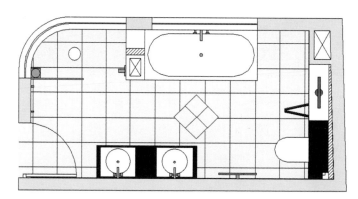

ABOVE: Floor plan

OPPOSITE: With a centrally located shower wall that's a shimmering, textured sculpture, there's no need to hang art on the walls.

GLASS SHOWER WALL:

The curved glass wall (from Fusion Glass) was created by pouring liquid laminated glass into sand; it was also tempered for toughness, an added safety measure. A curved stainless-steel frame was custom made to hold the glass in place. The curve made it tricky to get the frame right, and designer Tanya Hudson had to have it remade to ensure a proper fit. The outer surface of the glass wall is textured, but the inside is smooth, allowing for easy clean-up of water spots and scaling.

LIGHTING:

The recessed lighting in the shower is on a separate circuit from the rest of the bathroom, so it can be left on to shine into the living room, creating a diffused glow reminiscent of a glass lantern. The halogen fixtures are specially designed for use in a wet environment. The shower seems to double in size when its reflection appears in the copper paneling on the ceiling that abuts it. Angled lights in the ceiling are positioned to reflect against the glass to make it glow.

"The bathroom is quite a personal room for my clients," says the designer. "They really liked the idea of a library for the loo. You could spend hours in there reading a book, which makes it an indulgent experience." Amenities include a separate tub, twin sinks, wenge wood shelving for books, radiant floor heating under the limestone floors, and a wenge cabinet that is the room's sole storage unit and is large enough to hold a flat-screen television.

The double sinks are cantilevered from the walls, which required some planning. "There are no solid walls in new buildings," says Hudson, "so when you're going to hang sinks, you have to really plan it beforehand so you can hang them where there's a stud." By doing away with undersink cabinetry, she gave the room an uncluttered look. The generous, built-in wenge cabinet more than makes up for the lost storage,

as do the three illuminated mosaic-tiled niches, which are designed to be accessible from the shower and the bathtub.

To create a space that's warm and indulges all the senses, Hudson installed radiant floor heating underneath the creamy Portuguese limestone-tile floor and a sculptural towel-drying radiator on the wall by the sinks. Because the shower is open to the room, she slanted the whole floor toward the shower drain and waterproofed it with a lead lining. "There are lots of different ways to waterproof a floor, including rubber matting," she says. "I went with what the contractor had used before and was confident with." For an indulgent shower experience, she installed a wide showerhead with a thermostatic control that keeps the temperature constant. A ventilation system with two intake points handles the steam and moisture.

LEFT: A rainmaking showerhead provides plenty of water for an indulgent shower.

OPPOSITE: Although there is a lot of glass present in the bathroom's interior, the overall effect is of a warm, inviting place, which is ideal for the homeowners, who like to spend time relaxing with a book or watching television in the bath.

TUB AND TILE:

One-inch (2.5 cm) glass mosaic tiles by the Italian company Bisazza encase the partial wall between tub and shower and cover the wall that runs behind the tub. "The tiles are random standard colors," explains the designer. "You can also pick any colors you like. They create sheets by throwing them in a big vat, and out they come." The white bathtub from Bette is fitted with a polished-chrome Dornbracht faucet.

STORAGE:

A built-in custom wenge cabinet hides a television when it's not in use and provides storage for towels, cleaning supplies, and items usually kept in a medicine cabinet. Wenge shelves sealed with polyurethane offer lots of room for keeping books and magazines at hand; the dark, chocolatey wood makes a strong visual statement against the soft green of the glass panel behind the shelves. The bottom shelf is removable for easy system access.

SINKS:

A pair of white square porcelain sinks are cantilevered from the walls and fitted with high-arched Dornbracht faucets. Twin mirrors by H20 float over the sinks, while off to one side a sculptural polished-chrome radiator by Zehnder Yucca holds and warms towels.

MAKING THE MOST OF A HALF BATH

Although many people might find the small size of a half bath to be an obstacle to good design, Tanya Hudson, of the London firm Amok, sees it as an opportunity. "When you've got something so little," says the designer, "you can actually go quite mad and use a wild color you would never dare use in your living room. You can get away with it, and it makes it quite fun."

Some tips for designing a half bath:

GO MONOCHROME

In this half bathroom—"the disco loo," jokes Hudson—the walls are covered with Bisazza glass mosaic tiles in multiple hues of brown and gold. A black slate floor grounds the room and provides a strong visual counterpoint to the multiple browns. The only fixtures are a black toilet and a stainless-steel sink set into a black slate countertop. Using a single color unifies the disparate elements of the room, while the variations in hue add liveliness.

EMBRACE A BOLD COLOR

Paint the whole room—ceiling and walls—in a bold red or blue, so that you are really enveloped by the color. If it gets to be too much, you can always just close the door. Or if you leave it open, that vivid splash of color can provide an effective counterpoint to a more neutral decor.

CONSIDER THE LIGHTING

To increase natural light in a windowless room, borrow it from the outside hall by installing an opaque glass door, as was done in this half bath, or splurge on a skylight, if the space allows it. Overhead lighting can be enhanced with sconces or task lighting. This might be an area where playing with scale could be fun: Imagine a chandelier over the sink or tiny fairy lights twinkling around the mirror. And, of course, mirrors add light and a sense of space to a small room.

INVEST IN A FABULOUS MATERIAL

Interesting or beautiful materials can be quite costly, but where space is limited, you don't need large amounts. Splash out on hand-printed wallpaper, shimmering marble, gold leaf for the ceiling, or that honed granite counter you wish you could put in the kitchen. Sometimes leftovers can be purchased at showroom sales.

USE THE UNUSUAL

A small room is a good place to experiment: Sheathe the walls in mirror mosaic tiles or stainless-steel paneling, or make a backsplash of colorful acrylic or glass. MESH Architectures used a resin tile imbedded with white marble pebbles in one small half bath, then dramatized it by lighting the floor from below (see page 121). Or hire a plumber to transform an antique bucket, a wooden or copper bowl, or a favorite piece of pottery into a unique sink.

ACCESSORIZE

In a small space, the details are even more noticeable, so use sculptural towel rails, interestingly framed mirrors, or a great piece of art. "You want to create a space that feels good when you walk in," says Hudson. "You want it to be bright and warm."

ABOVE: The walls of this half bath, designed
by the London firm Amok, are tiled with
1" (2.5 cm) glass mosaic tiles in a random
pattern of browns and golds.

OPPOSITE: A polished-chrome faucet
with a single-lever handle serves the
small counter well.

TROPICAL TREATMENT

by Duccio Ermenegildo

"My designs are very much informed by how I like to live and what I consider luxuries," says Mexico-based designer Duccio Ermenegildo, who created this bath for a client's vacation home in Santo Domingo, Dominican Republic. The rest of the house is adorned with all the elements of a luxury seaside resort—complete with thatched roof pergolas and an infinity pool overlooking the ocean—but the master bathroom completes the dream with its soothing, creamy color palette and spacious floor plan.

"When people are on vacation, especially when they are by the sea, they love to take long showers and baths using oils and other spa amenities," says Ermenegildo. "Bathrooms have always been important in any kind of seaside getaway, and I put a lot of emphasis into creating alluring and attractive baths by making them as customized as possible."

Trained through the crash-course experience of designing his own home in Carreas, Mexico, Ermenegildo developed a technique for creating customized bathtubs from a porcelain-and-marble cement mixture poured into a form. All of his subsequent bathroom designs have incorporated this method—from tubs to sinks to flooring—which calls to mind a blend of Mediterranean and South American artisanal forms while feeling entirely tropical and distinctly Mexican.

In developing the material that shows up here—in not only the bathtub but on the floors and counter—Ermenegildo looked to the local craftsmen in Carreas. "My wife and I knew we wanted a very large tub in a fun, freestanding form, and none of the prefab options were deep enough," he explains. "It's also difficult to find imported marble or granite that isn't chipped or prohibitively expensive. I had seen the local guys working with a similar cement mixture for flooring, and I loved the soft, silken finish. Of course, there have been other custom cement bathtubs, but most need to be covered in swimming pool paint, and I thought there must be a way to achieve this effect without having to paint it."

The tub is 20" (50 cm) deep and 78" (200 cm) long. The pure white finish is achieved from equal parts of white porcelain cement (rather than sand or standard industrial cement), powdered marble, and white granite chips. The mixture is much like that used for terrazzo flooring. The granite chips give the material its structural integrity, but unlike the extensive sanding process used for terrazzo, which reveals shiny fragments of stone, this mixture is only finely hand-sanded to maintain a uniform shade and texture. "When smoothed with a fine trowel, the mortar has a patina that is almost like marble," says the designer.

Using the same material for the counters (through a somewhat more complicated technique when integrating the plumbing and fittings) and the floors, which were poured individually into 31 x 31" (80 x 80 cm) squares, the overall aesthetic of the space is soft and silky. A bonus: The cream-colored cement is cooling in the hot and humid climate of Santo Domingo, but it warms to the touch when getting in and out of a hot shower or bath.

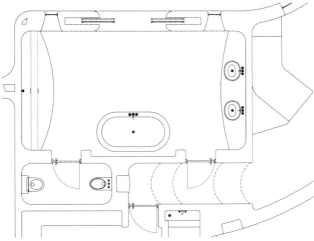

LEFT: Floor plan

OPPOSITE: This entirely customized bathroom uses carefully chosen, poured, all-white cement throughout: for the oversized bathtub for two, for the sink and vanity unit, and for the floors, which are embellished with a border of local sea pebbles.

MAHOGANY:

For the vanity, the designer used the same mahogany he used throughout the house but was careful to choose a woven design for the cabinet doors, which would allow for ventilation in the hot and humid climate of the Dominican Republic.

VANITY LIGHTING:

Duccio Ermenegildo positioned 600 watts of incandescent lighting behind a custom-designed mirror that is hung 6" (15.2 cm) from the wall. Controlled by a sophisticated electronic system, a variety of preset options allows for the lighting to range from warmly atmospheric to intense but indirect for applying makeup.

CEMENT:

Made from a white porcelain-and-granite cement mixture, the tub and sink were poured into a plywood mold, then sparingly waxed with standard Johnson's wax for a creamy finish. According to the designer, the wax is not necessary for sealing the material, which is water-proof when it sets, but imparts a warmer hue to the bright white cement.

For the shower area, Ermenegildo designated one entire wall of the space to be a wet area. Marked by a small, 2" (5.1 cm) step after a subtle border of sea pebbles, the floor of the shower area slopes toward a drain in the floor. "It's something that is best determined by the climate of the location. This bathroom dries very quickly, so it's not a problem for the floor to get wet," he says. "It's also warm enough that it feels okay to be showering in the open."

Encasing the plumbing in a spare beam of tropical hardwood that the designer imported from Mexico for the construction of the outdoor pergolas, the simple, oversized showerhead seems to grow right out of the Guayabillo tree. "I had an extra trunk of this wood hanging around after we'd completed the thatched-roof buildings, and I thought it would work perfectly in the bathroom," he explains. "We dug a canal in the center to run the plumbing through, and I installed a 12" (30.5 cm) solid-brass showerhead that I had carried on the plane back from Mexico—it weighed a ton, but I found what would normally be a $600 showerhead for only $30 at an industrial plumbing supply store in Mexico City."

Using a similar material on the walls to that which he had used throughout, the designer troweled the walls with a mixture of white marble and powdered cement. The result is an unbroken expanse of ivory-colored matte stucco from ceiling to floor. Windows and lighting com-plement this uniformity by appearing simply as cutouts in the walls fitted either with mahogany plantation shutters or discreet pocket doors.

"The only problem with these kinds of materials is that they are very labor intensive," says Ermenegildo. "Obviously, it takes much longer to do it this way than it does to set up a pre-fabricated bathtub. But I'm not particularly fond of the readymade fixtures out there, and this is the only way I've ever done it."

Of course, the benefit to a poured-to-perfection bathroom is that you can customize every little detail—embedding stones or other accents into the cement before it dries, carving details into the material, or staining and finishing it to your preference. Here the floors were poured into 31 x 31" (80 x 80 cm) squares as a way of adding some geometry to offset the prevalence of fluid, organic forms. The separately poured squares were also a practical choice because smaller spans of cement are less likely to crack than larger expanses, particularly in the fluctuating temperatures of a tropical climate. The designer created a customized border to the floor by embedding sea pebbles found on the nearby shore.

"The whole idea was to use the elements from the location and be inspired by the environment," says Ermenegildo, who used the same sea pebbles to make bronze casts for drawer pulls and hardware throughout the house.

OPPOSITE: The curved shower area is clean and simple with no doors or curtains to break up the space. An overhead beam of tropical Mexican hardwood envelops the shower plumbing, and simple fixtures and towel hooks keep things from feeling cluttered.

LEFT: In a tub big enough for two, the homeowners can enjoy a long soak surrounded by 6" (15.2 cm) of poured cement, which not only feels soft against the skin but keeps the water warm with its natural insulation. Standard Speakman tub fittings complete the simple but rustic look.

TROPICAL HARDWOOD:

Brought from Mexico for the construction of the outdoor thatched-roof pergolas, an extra trunk of Guayabillo wood supports the 12" (30.5 cm) showerhead that the designer found for $30 in a plumbing supply store in Mexico City.

SIMPLE STORAGE:

Customized niches nearly disappear into the walls and eliminate excess accessorizing. Standard wooden pegs hold towels out of range of the splash area but well within reach of a shower.

SEA PEBBLES:

Small stones found on the nearby seashore were embedded into the concrete to create a border around the perimeter of the flooring as well as to mark the entrance to the shower's wet area.

DESIGNER'S DREAM

by David Ling

When architect David Ling created a Design Idea Center for the National Kitchen and Bath Association's annual industry show (KBIS) in 2003, was doing more than dreaming up a luxurious virtual bath. In addition to designing a showroom on behalf of manufacturers Bisazza and Dornbracht, Ling was staging a dress rehearsal for the construction of a master bath underway in his own residence on Long Island, New York. Focusing on the beauty of the materials, he created a spatially innovative space that crossed the boundaries of a standard bathroom but was practical enough in its design to translate to a real bathroom with real walls.

With 250 sq ft (23.2 sq m) to work with, the architect divided the space into three separate zones, keeping in mind the materials and fixtures he wanted to use. True to his reputation for being able to make the industrial feel sublime, Ling picked styles from the sponsoring manufacturers that combined utilitarian simplicity with luxurious quality. "I knew I wanted shimmering mosaic tiles and knew which Dornbracht fixtures I wanted," he says. He combined four different styles of Bisazza tile: the enameled glass Opus Romano mosaic tile for the white floors and cobalt blue shower wall; slabs of black Logos terrazzo tile for the trough sink; Verticolor mosaic tile in red and lilac for the his-and-her toilet areas; and the luxurious Oro, which is made with white-gold leaf, for the backsplash. The sink and tub faucets are from Dornbracht's classic Tara line, which marries simple X's with a soft platinum finish. Fixtures from Duravit's Starck line complete the look of subdued luxury with their streamlined yet oversized dimensions.

Suggesting a his-and-her master bath floor plan, the architect chose an oversized bathtub (it can accommodate two people) along with a capacious curved shower wall, outfitted with both handheld and rainhead showers, along with eight body-spray nozzles. The trough sink, customized from sizeable slabs of Logos terrazzo tile, is one long, unbroken basin installed with two wall-mounted faucets for a modern take on a classic double vanity. In the toilet area, special his and hers zones are marked by two shades of mosaic tile: Red designates the woman's space, a grayish-lilac the man's. The result is a cohesive bath that marries functionality and style through zones designed for privacy and visual serenity.

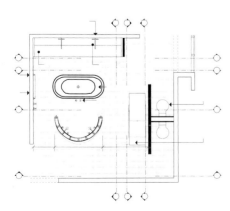

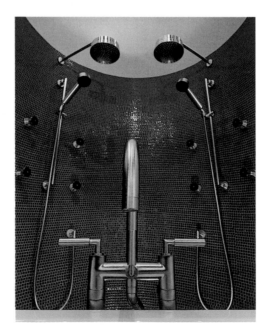

FAR LEFT: Floor plan

LEFT: For space that served as a "design idea" at the National Kitchen and Bath Industry Show, architect David Ling created an open-plan bath using four types of tile, each one marking a different zone.

OPPOSITE: In an open-plan bathroom created for a showroom but planned for his own residence, Ling made a large, curved, tiled wall the room's focal point. After covering it completely in lapis-colored glass mosaic tiles from Bisazza, he installed multiple showerheads for a shower area that functions as a spa treatment and looks like a work of art.

MULTIPLE SHOWERHEADS:
Combining two large-diameter showerheads with two handheld showers, all from Dornbracht, makes for a relaxing shower. Adding a total of eight adjustable heads along a curved tiled wall creates a blissful experience out of an everyday occurrence.

MOSAIC GLASS TILE:
Ling chose Opus Romano, an enameled glass ¾" (1.8 cm) square tile from Bisazza, normally used for commercial projects, for the striking white floors and undulating blue shower wall.

TUB:
Duravit's Starck 3 oversized bathtub is commodious enough for two. The third in a series of lines created by designer Philippe Starck for the company, the freestanding Starck 3 is built for comfort and has back-rests at both ends.

Taking his inspiration from a visit to Gala Placidia, a Byzantine mausoleum in Ravenna, Italy, Ling designed an arched wall for the shower that mimics the shape of a vaulted ceiling and then clad the entire wall in shiny blue mosaic tile. "I wanted curves," he explains. "At Gala Placidia, there were these lapis-blue double-vaulted ceilings accented with gold, and it was just incredible. I just really like curves. From there, I went with a kind of luxe minimalism."

To re-create the awe-inspiring effect of the Italian craftsmanship, he paired a similar shade of lapis blue with tiles in the backsplash that are backed with 24-karat white-gold leaf. "It's the most magical tile ever," he says of the Oro tile (the name means "gold" in Italian). "It's warm, and it's got a lot of depth because it has an uneven, mottled surface on the back. It's rough so they can adhere the gold to it, so it's almost the texture of a cleft stone. And it's completely handmade in Verona with three layers of gold leaf. They leaf it, laminate it, and then cut it." The result is a shimmering wall of silvery glass tiles facing a monolithic structure of slick, deep blue enamel set against a modern black-and-white background and accented with simple jewelrylike matte-finished fittings.

For the sink, the architect reimagined Bisazza's precast terrazzo tile, Logos, as an integral building material. He created a trough out of three large slabs of the black terrazzo for a clean-lined effect that contrasts nicely with the softly warped shower wall. Backed with the shimmering white-gold tile backsplash, the modern shape of the sink feels sturdy and permanent. Over the sink, a vanity mirror is broken up vertically with incandescent linear tubes that serve as task lighting for the vanity and as ambient lighting for the entire space. "These type of lights are commonly called linear incandescents," he says. "And they're great in a bathroom because they make skin tones look fabulous. When you dim incandescent light, it adds a kind of candlelight"—making it the ideal accent lighting for an evening soak or long shower.

Throughout the space, the architect contrasts subtle curves with straight lines and linear grids of square tiles. Organic shapes and natural elements are brought in with a pared-down selection of accessories in rich, dark wood from Calvin Klein. Otherwise, the showroom is a study in opposites: Mathematical curves with simple, clean, straight lines create a kind of syncopation through the space. The proof of a showroom's success, of course, is how well it can translate into real-life homes. For Ling, this practice has proved to be invaluable. "The design for my house is very similar," he explains. "It starts with that curved wall, but it's a little different now. It's still curvy, it's still blue, but it's going to be much more freeform and 60' (18.3 m) long. And now it swoops from the entrance, and goes down a hallway, and flows into a bedroom, and then becomes the shower wall."

LEFT: Ling created a dream bath by combining commercial-style lapis blue tile with black slabs of terrazzo and topping off the combination with a backsplash of mosaic tiles that get their shimmer from layers of 24-karat white-gold leaf, handmade by artisans in Verona, Italy.

OPPOSITE: Taking his cue from an ancient mausoleum in Ravenna, the architect paired lofty arches with deep blue tiles and touches of gold accents for a bathroom that takes the everyday experience to the extraordinary.

TROUGH SINK:

Made from slabs of precast terrazzo tile from Bisazza, the trough sink creates one long, uninterrupted line along the wall. By custom sizing for thickness, depth, and length, Ling was able to take a material traditionally used for floors or cladding and turn it into a fixture that integrates the form of the material with function.

FAUCET AND FITTINGS:

From Dornbracht's now-classic Tara line, the platinum finish on the faucets and shower temperature controls adds to the feeling of luxe minimalism: They are simple in their lines but extravagant in their quality and beauty.

DARK WOOD ACCESSORIES:

For a touch of nature, the architect brought in bath accessories from Calvin Klein. Adding warmth and neutral colors to the bold, slick atmosphere, the wood accents bring a dose of nature back to this sleek bathroom.

CONTRIBUTING ARCHITECTS AND INTERIOR DESIGNERS

MANUFACTURERS, SUPPLIERS, PRODUCTS, AND ONLINE RESOURCES

Please note that all phone numbers appear as they would be dialed in the country of their origin. You will need to consult a phone book for international country codes (and in some cases, city codes) and instructions for dialing overseas. The (o) represents a zero that is included when dialing within the country, but left off when dialing that number from overseas.

NORTH AMERICA

USA

Acrylite
Acrylic plastic is available in a wide range of colors at Canal Plastic Center, 345 Canal St., New York, NY 10013; Phone: 212-925-1032 and online at www.sdplastics.com.

Agape
Italian manufacturer of high-end bathroom fixtures, fittings, and accessories. For product information and showroom/dealer locations in the United States, see www.agapedesign.it.

American Olean
Company specializing in quality ceramic, glass, and stone tiles as well as tile accessories for the bath. For product information and showroom/dealer locations, see www.americanolean.com.

American Standard
Manufacturer of bath and kitchen products as well as air-conditioning and vehicle-control systems. For product information and dealer locations worldwide, see www.americanstandard.com.

Ann Sacks
Company specializing in fine tile and stone products as well as luxury plumbing products. For product and dealer information, see www.annsacks.com or call 800-278-8453.

Artemide
Email: artemide@artemide.us
Italian lighting company specializing in contemporary residential lighting. For product information and showroom/dealer locations in the United States, see www.artemide.com.

Bendheim Glass
61 Willett St.
Passaic, NJ 07055
Phone: 800-835-5304
(architectural division)
Website: www.bendheim.com
Direct importers and distributors of specialty glass, including architectural glass, restoration glass, and stained glass. (To the trade only.)

Bisazza
Website: www.bisazza.com
Italian company specializing in glass mosaic tiles. Bisazza tiles are available at the Home Depot, Expo, and other U.S. locations.

Emaux de Briare (in the United States)
86 Tec St.
Hicksville, NY 18801
Phone: 516-931-6925
French company specializing in decorative mosaic tiles. For product information and dealer locations, see www.emauxdebriare.com.

Chicago Faucets
Manufacturer of commercial and residential plumbing fixtures and fittings. For product information, see www.chicagofaucets.com.

Color Kinetics
Manufacturer of LED illumination technologies and related products; headquartered in Boston, Massachusetts, with offices in the Netherlands and China, and a joint venture in Japan. For product and contact information, see www.colorkinetics.com.

Dal-Tile
Manufacturer of a wide variety of ceramic, glass, and stone tiles. For product information and dealer locations, see www.daltile.com.

Design Source
115 Bowery
New York, NY 10002
Phone: 212-274-0022
Retailer of bathroom fixtures and fittings in a range of styles as well as decorative and architectural hardware.

Dornbracht
German manufacturer specializing in high-quality fittings and accessories for the bathroom and kitchen. For product information and showroom/dealer locations, see www.dornbracht.com.

Duravit
Manufacturer of quality bathroom fixtures and fittings. For product information, see www.duravit.com.

E-One Glass
630 U Ave.
Brooklyn, NY 11223
Phone: 718-812-8400
Owner Ivan Strachnyi is a designer and installer of residential and commercial glass, including shower doors and glass walls.

Elkay
Manufacturer of sinks, faucets, water coolers, drinking fountains, and kitchen accessories. For dealer locations in the United States, Canada, and Mexico, see www.elkay.com.

Fireslate
3065 Cranberry Hwy., Unit 24A
E. Wareham, MA 02538
Phone: 800-523-5902
Website: www.fireslate.com
Fireslate is a synthetic stone used to make fireplaces, flooring, counters, tabletops, desktops, and shelving.

Forbo Flooring, Inc.
P.O. Box 667
Humboldt Ind. Park
Hazleton, PA 18201
Phone: 570-459-0771;
toll free: 866-MARMOLEUM
Website:
www.themarmoleumstore.com

George Taylor Specialties
76 Franklin St.
New York, NY 10013
Phone: 212-226-5369
Supplier of sinks, tubs, toilets, and fixtures in a variety of styles.

Ginger
Manufacturer of fine bathroom accessories, lighting, and decorative hardware. For product information and dealer locations, see www.gingerco.com.

Grohe America, Inc.
241 Covington Dr.
Bloomingdale, IL 60108
Phone: 630-582-7711
Manufacturer specializing in faucets for bathrooms and kitchens. For product information and dealer locations, see www.groheamerica.com.

Hansgrohe
German manufacturer of shower, bathroom, and kitchen fixtures. Brands include Hansgrohe, Axor, and Pharo. For product information and dealer locations in the United States, see www.hansgrohe-usa.com.

Hastings Tile & Bath, Inc.
230 Park Ave. S.
New York, NY 10003
Phone: 212-674-9700
Website: www.hastingstilebath.com
Retailer of high-quality bath and tile products to designers, architects, builders, and homeowners.

Hettich
German company specializing in hardware for furniture, cabinets, and windows. For product and dealer information in the United States, see www.hettichamerica.com.

Home Depot EXPO Design Centers
For a location near you, see
www.expo.com.
The Home Depot of decorating has
something for every room of the house;
for bathrooms, there's everything from
fixtures, tiles, and lighting options to
furnishings, carpeting, and drapes.

Hydro Systems Whirlpool Baths
50 Moreland Rd.
Simi Valley, CA 93065
Phone: 805-584-9990
Email: sales@hydrosystem.com
Website: www.hydrosystem.com
Manufacturer of quality bathtubs,
whirlpool baths, and accessories.

Jacuzzi
Manufacturer of quality whirlpool
baths, spas, shower systems,
and other fixtures for bathrooms
and kitchens.
For product information and showroom
locations in the United States, see .
www.jacuzzi.com or call 800-288-4002.

Kallista
Manufacturer of quality bathroom
fixtures, fittings, and accessories,
along with designer suites of bathroom
furniture by Barbara Barry and
Michael S. Smith.
For product information and showroom
locations in the United States, see
www.kallista.com.

Kohler
Manufacturer of quality fixtures and
fittings for bathrooms and kitchens.
For product information and
showroom/dealer locations in the
United States, see www.us.kohler.com.

Kroin
Kroin was for many years the U.S.
importer of the Vola line, which it
sold under the Kroin name. See Vola
contact information.

Live Tile
121 McKinley Ave.
Hawthorne, NJ 07506
Phone: 973-636-9199
Email: livetileusa@msn.com
Website: www.livetileusa.com
Manufacturer of specialty glass
tiles made of 100% non-recycled
"float" glass. (To the trade only.)

Lumicor
Lumicor is represented to the A/D
community in the United States by
The Designtex Group. Architects and
designers can call 800-221-1540 or
Email: sales@dtex.com.
Website: www.lumicor.com
Manufacturer of translucent acrylic
resin panels encapsulating textiles,
metals, papers, and foliage.
(To the trade only.)

Nanz Custom Hardware, Inc.
20 Vandam St.
New York, NY 10013
Phone: 212-367-7000
Website: www.nanz.com
Manufacturer of high-end hardware,
such as knobs, levers, locks,
and window and cabinet hardware,
for the home.

Newport Brass
Website: www.newportbrass.com
Subsidiary of BrassTech, a
manufacturer of designer plumbing
fixtures and fittings for kitchens,
bathrooms, and bars.

NUHEAT
Manufacturer of electric heating
system for stone and tile floors.
For product information and dealer
locations, see www.nuheat.com

Oregon Hinoki Products
Website: www.malalla.net/ohp
Online supplier of hinoki cedar and
builder of Japanese soaking tubs,
stools, and other accessories.

Porcher
Manufacturer of a wide range of
fixtures, fittings, furniture, and
accessories for bathrooms.
For product information and
showroom/dealer locations, see
www.porcher-us.com
or call 866-455-6118, ext. 1059.

Panelite (sales office)
600 Broadway, Suite 4C
New York, NY 10012
Phone: 212-343-0995
Phone (in LA): 310-202-1115
Website: www.e-panelite.com
Manufacturer of lightweight,
translucent panels used for doors,
walls, furniture, and floors.

Pharo (see Hansgrohe)

Restoration Resources, Inc.
Bill Raymer, owner
31 Thayer St.
Boston, MA 02118
Phone: 617-542-3033
Website: http://members.aol.com/
wcrres/index.htm
Small company specializing in
independent architectural antique
salvage of items such as hardware,
lighting, and interior and exterior
architectural decor.

Riverstone
Riverstone tiles are available through
Artistic Tile (for showroom/dealer
locations, call 800-260-8646 or see
www.artistictile.com).

Santa & Cole
Spanish manufacturer of high-end
lighting for the home.
For product information and dealer
location, see www.santacole.com.

Six-Eleven Limited
11921 Sherman Way
North Hollywood, CA 91605
Phone: 818-982-9546
Manufacturer of high-end
custom bathtubs.

Stanley Works
Manufacturer of tools, hardware,
doors, pneumatic tools and fasteners,
automatic doors, storage systems,
and more.
For product and distributor
information, see
www.stanelyworks.com.

Starphire
Starphire glass is available through
various suppliers, including Panorama
City Glass (14621 Arminta St.,
Van Nuys, CA 91402, USA;
Phone: 010-780 0637].
For more information, see
www.ppg.com/gls_commercial/
products/starphire.asp.

Stone Soup Concrete
221 Pine St.
Florence, MA 01062
Phone: 413-582-0783;
toll-free: 800-819-3456
Email: info@StoneSoupConcrete.com
Website: www.stonesoupconcrete.com

Sunrise Specialty Company
930 98th Ave.
Oakland, CA 94603
Phone: 510-729-7277
Manufacturer of quality
antique-style bathtubs and fittings.
For product and distributor
information, see
www.sunrisespecialty.com.

Syndecrete
Precast concrete made with recycled
aggregates, developed by architect
David Hertz. For more information, see
www.syndesisinc.com.

Urban Archaeology
143 Franklin St.
New York, NY 10013
Phone: 212-431-4646
Company specializing in bathroom
fixtures, fittings, accessories, and
lighting inspired by historic designs,
as well as handmade mosaics,
tile, and stone.
For product information and
location of additional showrooms, see
www.urbanarchaeology.com.

Vermont Structural Slate
3 Prospect St.
Fair Haven, VT 05743
Phone: 800-343-1900
Fabricator of natural slate and stone
products for flooring, roofing, and
other architectural uses.

Vitra
29 Ninth Ave.
New York, NY 10014
Phone: 212-929-3626
www.vitra.com

Vola (U.S. importer)
Hastings Tile and Il Bagno Collection
30 Commercial St.
Freeport, NY 11520
Phone: 800-351-0038
Email: vola@hastings30.com
Danish manufacturer of Arne
Jacobsen–designed kitchen and
bath fittings and accessories.
For more product information, see
www.vola.dk.

Walker Zanger
Company specializing in quality
natural stone and crafted ceramic,
metal, and glass tiles.
For product information and
showroom/dealer locations, see
www.walkerzanger.com
or call 800-761-0577.

Waterworks
Company specializing in high-quality
kitchen and bath fixtures and fittings,
as well as surfaces (ceramic, glass,
and mosaic tiles), furnishings, and
accessories.
For product information and showroom
locations, see www.waterworks.com
or call 800-927-2120.

Whitehaus Collection
Company specializing in bathroom
fixtures, fittings, and accessories,
including the Nymphaea basin,
which changes color according to
water temperature.
For more product information and
dealer locations, see
www.whitehauscollection.com
or call 800-527-6690.

Wilsonart International
Website: www.wilsonart.com
Manufacturer of decorative
surfacing products such as
laminates and flooring.

Zimmer + Rohde
Website: www.zimmer-rohde.com
Textile manufacturers of three
distinct fabric lines: Ardecora, Etamine,
and Zimmer + Rohde.

CANADA

Eurolite
5 Lower Sherbourne St.
Toronto, Ontario M5A 2P3
Phone: 416-203-1501
Retailer of contemporary
lighting products from Europe
and North America.

Ginger's Bath
95 Ronald Ave.
Toronto, Ontario M6E 5A2
Phone: 416-787-1787
Retailer of bathroom fixtures,
fittings, and accessories in a range
of styles; carries products by Kohler,
Ultrabath, and Vola.

Grohe Canada, Inc.
1226 Lakeshore Rd. E.
Mississauga, Ontario L5E 1E9
Phone: 905-271-2929
Manufacturer specializing in faucets
for bathrooms and kitchens.
For product information and dealer
locations in Canada, see
www.groheamerica.com.

Häfele
Supplier of hardware for cabinets
and furniture as well as bath
accessories.
For distributors in Canada, the
United States, and Mexico, see
www.hafeleonline.com.

Kallista
Manufacturer of quality bathroom
fixtures, fittings, and accessories, as
well as designer suites of bathroom
furniture by Barbara Barry and
Michael S. Smith.
For product information and
showroom locations in Canada, see
www.kallista.com.

Kohler
Manufacturer of quality fixtures and
fittings for bathrooms and kitchens.
For product information and show-
room/dealer locations in Canada, see
www.us.kohler.com/wheretobuy/search
_location.jsp.

Lumicor
Lumicor is represented to the A/D
community in Canada by Richelieu
Hardware Ltd.
Canadian architects and designers
can call 866-832-4060 or Email:
info@richelieu.com
Website: www.lumicor.com
Manufacturer of translucent,
acrylic-resin panels encapsulating
textiles, metals, papers, and foliage.

Majestic Fireplaces
Website: www.majesticfireplaces.com

RJW Enterprises
19 Industrial Blvd.
Parry Sound, Ontario P2A 2W8
Phone: 888-279-7841
Email: bob_rjw@cogeco.net
Manufacturer of "Cecconi Simone II"
(custom Corian Sink that is lit from
within).

Stone Tile
1451 Castlefield Ave.
Toronto, Ontario M6M 1Y3
Phone: 416-515-9000
Retailer of imported high-quality natural stone products and ceramic tile
from around the world.

Thermoveil Shadecloths 1000 Series
available through Sunproject Shading
Systems (for locations throughout
Canada, see www.sunproject.com).

Ultra Baths or BainUltra
Phone: 800-463-2187
Email: info@BainUltra.com
Websites: www.bainultra.com and
www.ultrabaths.com
Manufacturer of the Thermo-masseur
bathtub and accessories.

EUROPE

Agape
Italian manufacturer of high-end bathroom fixtures, fittings, and accessories.
For product information and show-
room/dealer locations in Europe, see
www.agapedesign.it.

Artemide
Italian lighting company specializing in
contemporary residential lighting.
For product information and show-
room/dealer locations throughout
Europe, see www.artemide.com.

Aston-Matthews Ltd
141-147a Essex Rd.
London N1 2SN
UK
Phone: (0)20 7226 7220
Website: www.astonmatthews.co.uk
Retailer specializing in bathroom fix-
tures, fittings, and accessories.

Bisazza
Italian company specializing in glass
mosaic tiles.
For product information and show-
room/dealer locations worldwide, see
www.bisazza.com.

Gres de Breda
Spanish tile company.
For production information and loca-
tions, see www.grupobreda.com.

Emaux de Briare
7 rue de Bac
75007 Paris
France
Phone: 42 61 16 41
French company specializing in
decorative mosaic tiles.
For product and dealer information,
www.emauxdebriare.com.

The Conran Shop
Michelin House
81 Fulham Rd.
London SW3 6RD
UK
For other locations in London, Paris,
New York, Tokyo, and Fukuoka, Japan,
see www.conran.com.

Dornbracht
German manufacturer specializing
in high-quality fittings and accessories
for the bathroom and kitchen.
For product information and
showroom/dealer locations, see
www.dornbracht.com.

Fusion Glass
Phone: (0)20 7738 5888
Website: www.fusionglass.co.uk
Company specializing in the
creation and installation of
architectural, structural, and
decorative glass products.

Hansgrohe
German manufacturer of shower,
bathroom, and kitchen fixtures. Brands
include Hansgrohe, Axor, and Pharo.
For product information and dealer
locations in Europe, see
www.hansgrohe.com.

C.P. Hart
Bathroom and kitchen showrooms:
Newnham Terrace
Hercules Rd.
London SE1 7DR
UK
Phone: (0)20 7902 1000

103-105 Regents Park Rd.
Primrose Hill
London NW1 8UR
UK
Phone: (0)20 7586 9856
English company specializing in
designer bathroom and kitchen
fixtures and fittings.
For U.K. locations outside of London,
see www.cphart.co.uk.

Hettich International
Vahrenkampstraße 12-16
32278 Kirchlengern
Germany
Phone: (0)5223 / 77-0
Email: info@de.hettich.com
Website: www.hettich.com
German company specializing in
hardware for furniture, cabinets,
and windows.

Hollys of Bath
Website: www.hollysofbath.com
English manufacturer of quality,
antique-style fittings and accessories
for bathrooms and kitchens.

The Kelly Hoppen Shop
175-177 Fulham Rd.
London SW3 6JW
UK
Phone: (0)20 7351 1910

Kallista
Manufacturer of quality bathroom
fixtures, fittings, and accessories, as
well as designer suites of bathroom
furniture by Barbara Barry and
Michael S. Smith.
For product information and
showroom locations in Europe, see
www.kallista.com.

Kohler
Manufacturer of quality fixtures and
fittings for bathrooms and kitchens.
For product information and show-
room/dealer locations in Europe, see
www.us.kohler.com/wheretobuy/
search_location.jsp.

Myson
Manufacturer of radiators
and towel warmers.
For product information and locations,
see www.myson.co.uk or call customer
service in the U.K. at (0)191 4917530.

Rapsel Studio
Italian company specializing in
designer bathroom fixtures and fittings.
For product information and dealer
locations worldwide, see
www.rapsel.it.

Santa & Cole (main offices)
Balmes 71
E 08440 Cardedeu
Spain
Phone: 937 017 110
Email: info@santacole.com
Spanish manufacturer of high-end
lighting for the home.
For product information and dealer
location, see www.santacole.com.

SICIS Mosaic & Art
Italian company specializing
in mosaic tiles.
For product information and
showroom/dealer locations, see
www.sicis.com.

Vola UK Ltd.
Unit 12, Ampthill Business Park
Station Road, Ampthill
Bedfordshire MK45 2QW
UK
Phone: (0)1525 84 11 55
Email: sales@vola.co.uk
Website: www.vola.co.uk
Danish manufacturer of Arne
Jacobsen–designed kitchen and bath
fittings and accessories.
For more distributors throughout
Europe, see www.vola.dk.

Zehnder Yucca
Zehnder Heizkörper AG
Oberfeldstrasse 2
5722 Gränichen
Switzerland
Phone: 62 855 11 11
Email: mail@zehnder.net
Website: www.zehnder-heizkoerper.ch
Swiss company specializing in
high-design radiated towel bars.

ASIA

Agape
Italian manufacturer of high-end
bathroom fixtures, fittings,
and accessories.
For product information and
showroom/dealer locations in Asia, see
www.agapedesign.it.

Cera Trading Company
Retailer of European and U.S.
bathroom fixtures (including Vola); also
developer and manufacturer of recent
line of original products.
For product information and dealer
locations in Japan, see www.cera.co.jp.

Hansgrohe
German manufacturer of shower,
bathroom, and kitchen fixtures. Brands
include Hansgrohe, Axor, and Pharo.
For product information and dealer
locations in Asia, see
www.hansgrohe.com.

INAX fixtures and fittings
Japanese manufacturer of fixtures and
fittings for kitchens and bathrooms,
as well as a range of tile products.
For product information, see
www.inax.co.jp.

Kohler
Manufacturer of quality fixtures and
fittings for bathrooms and kitchens.
For product information and
showroom/dealer locations in Asia, see
www.us.kohler.com/wheretobuy/
search_location.jsp.

Vola (Hong Kong importer)
Portfolio Group Limited
G/F, 59 Elgin St.
Central, Hong Kong
Phone: 28680765
Email: sales@pgltd.com.hk

Vola (Tokyo importer)
Fuji Design Corp.
3-15-14 Higashi-Ikebukuro
Toshima-ku, Tokyo 170-0013
Phone: 3983-2251
Email: inf@fujid.com
Website: www.fujid.com

PHOTOGRAPHER CREDITS

Abramson Teiger Architects, 5 (plan); 76

Amok Ltd., 154

Jon Anderson Design Service, 130; 133 (bottom)

Archisis, Inc., 50

Austin Patterson Disston Architects, 134 (left)

©Berridge Kirchner Floorplans, 128 (right)

Björg/Chelsea Atelier Architects, 109; 110; 113

Andrew Bordwin/Delson or Sherman Architects, 84; 85 (top); 87

Andrew Bordwin/Henry Mitchell Interior Architecture, 93; 95

Andrew Bordwin/Wayne Nathan Design, 107

The CALLA Companies, 88; 91

Cecconi Simone, Inc., 62

Benny Chan/Fotoworks, 52; 53

Winston Brock Chappell, Architect, 46

Chelsea Atelier Architect, 108; 112

John Colamarino, Architect, 7 (right); 105 (right)

ColePrévost, Inc., 98; 102

Delson or Sherman Architect, 85 (bottom); 86

DesignArc, 150

Carlos Domenech, 39 (bottom)

Carlos Domenech/Living Interior Design, 140 (left); 141

Duccio Ermenegildo, 160

Elizabeth Felicella/Beyer Blinder Belle, Architects, 5; 143

Elizabeth Felicella/Amelie Rives Rennolds, Architect, 30

Elizabeth Felicella/Urban Archaeology, 10

Michael Freeman/N Maeda Atelier, 120; 121 (bottom)

Michael Freeman/Toshihiko Suzuki, Architect, 149

Tria Giovan/JS Creations, Inc., 64 (right); 65; 66; 67

Tria Giovan/Betty Wasserman Art & Interiors Ltd., 79; 80; 81

William Hefner Architecture and Interiors, 54 (right)

©Dave Henderson/The CALLA Companies, 2; 89; 90

©Dave Henderson/Jon Anderson Design Service, 131; 132; 133 (top)

Mark Hutker & Associates Architects, Inc., 122

JS Creations, Inc., 64 (left)

Kanner Architects, 69

Glenn Leitch, Architect, 78

Di Lewis/Elizabeth Whiting & Associates, 56; 58 (right); 59

John Edward Linden/Studio Ethos, 96; 97 (top)

David Ling, Architect, 164 (left)

David Ling, Architect/Courtesy of Dornbracht & Bisazza, 7 (left); 164 (right); 165; 166; 167

Living Interior Design, 140 (right)

Mark Lohman/Abramson Teiger Architects, 72; 73; 74; 77

Mark Lohman/William Hefner Architecture and Interiors, 54 (left); 55

N Maeda Atelier, 121 (top)

Peter Malinowski/DesignArc, 151; 152; 153

Jeff McNamara/Austin Patterson Disston Architects, 134 (right); 135

MESH Architectures, 116; 119; 144; 146

Henry Mitchell Interior Architecture, 94

Cristian Molina/ColePrévost, Inc., 40; 99; 100; 101; 103

Eduardo Muñoz/The Interior Archive, 128 (left); 129

Frank Oudeman/MESH Architectures, 115; 117; 118; 147

Peter Romaniuk, Architect, 58 (left)

Michael Scates/Amok, 43; 155; 156; 157; 158; 159

Bob Shimer, Hedrich Blessing/Courtesy of Elliott + Associates, 21

Fred Stocker/Winston Brock Chappell, Architect, 45; 47; 49

Fred Stocker/Kanner Architects, 68; 70

Tim Street-Porter/Archisis, Inc., 51

Tim Street-Porter/Duccio Ermenegildo, 161; 162; 163

Studio Ethos, 97 (bottom)

Toshihiko Suzuki, Architect, 148

Van Dam and Renner Architects, 139

Brian Vanden Brink/John Colamarino, Architect, 104; 105 (left)

Brian Vanden Brink/ Mark Hutker & Associates Architects, Inc., 123; 124; 126; 127

Brian Vanden Brink/Steven M. Foote, FAIA, Perry Dean Rogers Partners, 8

Brian Vanden Brink/William Pierce Interiors, Inc., 13

Brian Vanden Brink/Van Dam and Renner Architects, 137; 138

Joy von Tiedemann/Cecconi Simone, Inc., 61; 63; 83

ABOUT THE AUTHORS

Holly Harrison is a freelance writer and editor specializing in art and design. She has contributed to numerous magazines, including *Metropolitan Home*, and is the author of *Altered Books, Collaborative Journals, and Other Adventures in Bookmaking* and *Collage for the Soul: Expressing Hopes and Dreams Through Art*. She and her husband live in Concord, MA.

Interior design writer and editor **Sarah Lynch** is the author of *77 Habits of Highly Creative Interior Designers*, *The Perfect Room*, and *Modern Color*. She has written for several high-profile magazines including *Metropolitan Home*.

ACKNOWLEDGMENTS

We would like to thank the talented group of architects and designers who contributed so much to this project by sharing with us their insights and experience as well as their beautiful designs.

To the many manufacturers and retailers who contributed photography for Section One, allowing us to present a wide array of new products and materials, we are grateful.

Many people at Rockport Publishers contributed to the successful completion of this project: Sarah Chaffee, Pamela Elizian, Cora Hawks, David Martinell, Stoltze Design, and our editor, Mary Ann Hall. A special thank you is reserved for Betsy Gammons, our photo editor, who had the idea for this book, provided endless inspiration, and was tireless in her efforts to track down photography, floor plans, and at least a dozen other important details.